Millions Now Living
A book of Kingdom Maladies
By Unky Punky

My thanks goes out to every person that contributed to this book. Names have been changed to protect the identities of those taking part. I hope this work is helpful to all those interested in the lives of Jehovah's witnesses. I am confident that it is an accurate portrayal of what life is really like in the Watchtower corporation, even when related in fun. The portrayals come from first hand experience.

Likeness to anyone living or zombie is a miracle.

Cartoons © Punk 2015
Book © Paul G Jackson 2015

cover by Punkofnice
Millions Now Living

The Unky Punky and friends guide to the Jehovah's witness world.

Obligatory intro - Knock, knock. Who's there?

I am told that a supposed 'wise man' said: "..of making many books *there is* no end; and much study is a weariness of the flesh." **Ecclesiastes 12:12.**

Ironically, his words are written in a book. That book being the Bible, of course. The Bible is a religious book, among many other religious books and writings.

There are an estimated 4,200 religions in the world. One of those, is a religion that I was associated with from birth, Jehovah's witnesses.

I'm not going to go into detailed origins, history or beliefs of the 'JWs'. I hope that the following pages will provide all the insights needed.

I have included a 'glossary' of Jehovah's witness phrases, words and jargon. To balance this, I have included a glossary of ironic terms often used by non or ex Jws, in relation to the Watchtower corporation. Neither glossary is exhaustive. It would be exhausting to make an exhaustive one.

Right from the start, this book is not pushing any religious/atheistic agenda. It simply includes interviews with people associated with Jehovah's witnesses. It is also meant to be humorous and ironic but not malicious.

For the interviews, I merely wish to set before the reader, the opinions of people. However, this can be an emotive subject, so expect some open and honest remarks. Therefore, the objective of this work is to give voice to anyone that has had dealings in or out of the Jehovah's Witness faith.

'Diehard and Doubting' are not characters. These cartoons are representative of situations.

The other objective is just to enjoy some light heartedness.

Read with an open mind. Get your popcorn ready and enjoy!

Kind regards,
Unky Punky, Cambridge, UK. 2015.

Section 1: The Interviews.

Section 2: Tales and other things.

Section 3: Glossary of JW terms and ironic terms.

Section 1

THE INTERVIEWS

Introducing the interviewees:

Name or preferred pseudonym : **Flipper**
Gender : Male
Country : USA
Were/are you a JW ? I was a JW - past tense. Now an EX-JW.
How were/are you associated with JWs? Born in.
How long were you a JW ? 44 years from birth until age 44.

Paula Mewies
Female
Wales, UK
Were/are you a JW ? 2 weeks away from baptism after 4 years study.
How were/are you associated with JWs? A Bible student. They knocked at my door, bless them.
How long were you a JW ? 4.5 years study total.

Kurt Grenzelos
Male
Germany
Were/are you a JW ? Reluctantly.
How were/are you associated with JWs? Forced as a child by my mentally ill mother.
How long were you a JW ? 35 years. 12 years from baptism.

Natalia
Female
UK
Were/are you a JW ? Would be considered a JW but do not feel in my heart or head that I am actually one. Do not go out on the ministry, absolutely hate it so I would be

considered 'inactive' I guess.
How were/are you associated with JWs? Born in.
How long were you a JW ? Born to JW parents (although one parent disassociated and now a non-believer). Baptised at 15. Left for a brief period of time in very early 20's, then was on the way back in when I realised it's not right and struggling to get out.

Spiral Blue
Female
USA
Were/are you a JW ? Yes.
How were/are you associated with JWs? Pretty much born in, my mother was studying when I was little and she was baptized when I was 6.
How long were you a JW ? From 13 (baptized) to 45, 32 years. Out mentally for awhile before that.

Eve Farady (at least this is the English version of my birth name so this will do. Smiles.
Female
Hungary
Were/are you a JW ? Yes.
How were/are you associated with JWs? They came to my door.
How long were you a JW ? I was studying on and off for about 5 years. Then, I was an active witness for 14 years, inactive for 3 years. I disassociated myself about 2 months ago.

Marcus
Male
UK
Were/are you a JW ? Unbaptised publisher 1990. Faded soon after.
How were/are you associated with JWs? Born in.
How long were you a JW ? Never really was at heart.

Sazzle
Female
UK
Were/are you a JW ? Unbaptized publisher.
How were/are you associated with JWs? Brought up in the religion.
How long were you a JW ? I was going to meetings until 15 years old.

Catherine Coyle Murphy
Female
USA Midwest
Were/are you a JW ? I was.
How were/are you associated with JWs? Studied with jws and became one at age 21. I was disassociated by actions.

Gracie
Female
Los Angeles, CA, USA
Were/are you a JW? No.   So far I haven't studied with them either. I am actually kicking around the idea of starting to study with them, so I can have more opportunities to try and plant seeds of doubt. Right now, I am busy with work and tutoring family etc etc. I don't have time to try and do that. If I do start to study with them, it will be purely to try and plant seeds. If I do this, I am going to seek out members who aren't born in. I am also going to seek out young adults between 18-25 who are trying to get out. I tutor a lot of college subjects, so I was actually thinking of maybe, volunteering my services to JW students and then help encourage them to leave, by getting their degree.
Yes, I know shunning from a family is very painful. I also know for some, they'd rather leave, even if it means their family will shun them. I have become very aware of the fact that anybody who leaves the JWs, or any cult for that matter, need a very strong emotional support system in place. I am kicking around the idea of tutoring, and then if the subject comes up, well, take it from there. Right now, it seems like I am still a little too busy to get something started. It's actually too bad Bible Studies can't be conducted from midnight to 2am. (laughs). Or are they??
How were/are you associated with JWs? Via friend/s. My friend is currently studying with them.

Mandy Brennan
Female
UK
Were/are you a JW? Was a JW
How were/are you associated with JWs? I joined from personal choice
How long were you a JW? 10 years

Angus Robertson
Male
UK
Were/are you a JW? Yes, I was.
How were/are you associated with JWs? I was born in

How long were you a JW? Born in. Baptised at 17. Left at age 42

Robyn
Female
Scotland
Were/are you a JW? Yes, I was.
How were/are you associated with JWs? Kinda - born in, raised from the age of 4. It was all I ever knew.
How long were you a JW? From the age of 4 till I was 19, so roughly 15 years

Julia Douglas
Female
Canada
Were/are you a JW? I was raised as one of Jehovah's Witnesses since I was an infant, when my mother converted. I left in 2009.
How were/are you associated with JWs? Born in. Baptized at 14. Disfellowshipped at 36
How long were you a JW? 36 years or counting from baptism; 22 years.

Locutus
Male
Canada
Were you a JW? Yes. Born in.
How were/are you associated with JWs? Born in, unbaptised.
How long were you a JW? 18 years.

Jason Thickpenny
Male
UK
Were you a JW? Yes.
How were/are you associated with JWs? Born in.
How long were you a JW? Born in. Baptised at 14. Left at 23.

Paul Unky Punky
Male
UK
Were/are you a JW ? I was a JW. Not anymore.
How were/are you associated with JWs? Born in. Baptised in 1973 when I was only 15. Too young to vote and do other adult things. I was therefore, essentially underage. However, no one in the watchtower corporation objected. Even underage, the Watchtower corporation can punish you as if you were an adult.
How long were you a JW ? Until I woke up to the illogical nature of it all in 2010. I was 52. A little while after that, I stopped going to the meetings. The Elders decided to forcibly, disassociate me; kick me out, because I went to a church on a few occasions. Thanks to the rules of the Watchtower corporation, this broke up my family. Something they claim they never do!

One Eyed Joe
Male
USA
Were/are you a JW ? I was a JW, but no longer consider myself to be one.
How were/are you associated with JWs? Born in.
How long were you a JW ? 28 years.

Louise Goode
Female
UK

Were/are you a JW ? I was a JW
How were/are you associated with JWs? Born in.
How long were you a JW ? 30 years.

Mickey Hudson/Danmera
Female
USA
Were/are you a JW ? Was, but never baptised. Even though I was never baptised, I believed the Watchtower to be "the truth", until my 40s.
How were/are you associated with JWs? Basically, mom joined when I was just a toddler.
How long were you a JW ? From toddler to leaving the physical part of the organisation, in my early 20s. Even though I left the physical part of the Watchtower organisation, I didn't leave mentally until my 40s.

SailAway
Female
USA
Were/are you a JW? Yes, I was a JW.
How were/are you associated with JWs? My father accepted a family study when I was nine years old. By age 10 I became an unbaptized publisher. My entire family stopped studying with the witnesses within two years, but I stayed in and was baptized at age 16 in 1975 with my father's permission.
How long were you a JW? 42 years

Village Idiot
Male
USA
Were/are you a JW? Yes I was. No longer.
How were/are you associated with JWs? Born in? Thank goodness no. Baptized in 1974. Joined from personal choice. Yeap, that's me. Via friends.
How long were you a JW? 8 years.

Reopened Mind
Female
USA
Were/are you a JW ? I was a JW.

How were/are you associated with JWs? Via friend/s. I began studying with two girls in school when I was 14/15 years old. That was in the 60s, when

the "Truth" book had come out. There was the pressure to get baptized after six months of study. But because I was a minor living at home with parents who didn't like JWs they agreed to keep me as a study. I left home and was baptized at 20.
How long were you a JW? 38 years.

Sue/SG75
Female
USA
Were/are you a JW? Yes, I was a JW.
How were/are you associated with JWs? My mother first met JWs when we lived on Camp Lejeune where my father was a Marine, in the early 80s. I was five at the time. Mom got baptized after Dad was discharged and we moved back to Pennsylvania.
How long were you a JW? 20 years.

What drew you to the JWs?

Flipper: My JW parents - I had no choice. They joined 8 years before I was born. As a teenager I truly was deceived and believed in a " Paradise " and " living forever " - thought it sounded great - until I found out it was a lie.

Paula: Kindness, love, friendship, part of 'something else', loved me 'whatever'.

Kurt: My mother forced me to attend.

Natalia: Didn't have a choice. Was raised going to meetings, conventions, assemblies and going out in the ministry. Father became an Ministerial Servant and eventually an Elder. Felt it was 'the truth' long after my Father left.

Spiral: Forced, or "stuck" as a child. Stayed with it later because of family and friends.

Eve: They were friendly and I had problems at the time in my family life, which I felt they could help me with. I loved the family book. I was not interested at first, in theoretical questions (like trinity).

Marcus: I was raised in the cult. It wasn't a choice I made. If I was able to have made a choice before birth I would have had nothing to do with this dangerous high control cult.

Sazzle: I had no choice. My parents were JW and I was forced to be part of their religion.

Catherine: Met one at work and got in to it that way. Was one for 30 years.

Gracie: Not applicable.

Mandy: I liked the idea of a paradise and on the initial Bible study I took, everything made sense. The JWs used the scriptures all the time, and at meetings people were kind and friendly. The children were well behaved

Angus: I stayed in for social reasons, married in the cult and it became my routine.

Robyn: Nothing drew me, I had no choice, but I could say what drove my mother. She was in a long term abusive relationship with my father in England. Her mum had just died and her sister was an active JW up in Scotland. She came to Scotland with me and my sister to get away from her tumultuous life, and took refuge with her sister the JW. She started studying and attending meetings, met my adoptive father and was baptised and married within the year. I can say with much conviction, that she was cherry picked from what was a terrible situation, targeted as a vulnerable person and brainwashed into thinking it was the only positive life choice she could make.

Julia: Well, I was raised as a JW but I grew to believe it was 'the Truth' and didn't want to be destroyed at Armageddon.

Locutus: Born in, Family also all in for generations.

Jason: Being born in, I knew nothing other than the JW's. It was a case of "All JW's are good, all who are not are bad". Being indoctrinated with that from the time you can talk, means no friends outside the JW's. Therefore, I hated everyone who wasn't a JW – *because that how was trained to think.* Being honest, I carried through up till I left. They created me a bubble and I was "happy" to float around in it.

Paul: Nothing drew me to the filth. If anything, a lot repulsed me as I grew up but I ignored it. After all, this was supposed to be the one true religion. I was raised in the cult. I had no choice.

Joe: My parents required it.

Louise: Born in

Danmera: It was all I knew, and I was taught everything else was wrong. It wasn't anything that "drew" me, it just was.

SailAway: The witnesses target vulnerable, idealistic people. I was drawn in by their promise of a happy family life. My mother was/is mentally ill and my father was an alcoholic and serial cheater who couldn't keep a job. We were at times homeless.

Village Idiot: All it took was a tract on the door. I was 13 and naive and had an interest in religion. I thought I was discovering the secrets of the Universe.

Reopened Mind: Believe it or not, that they would change their doctrines. At the time, I thought that was because as they realized something was wrong, they would correct it. They also projected themselves as one big happy family. Living in a paradise earth with no death, disease, war, or other problems appealed to my idealistic teenage self.

Sue: I didn't have a choice. Mom took us to meetings and Dad didn't stop her. I was baptized at 14 because that's what I thought was expected of me.

What do/did you enjoy about being a JW?

Flipper: Nothing whatsoever.

Paula: Being part of a group. Knowing about the 'truth', when the 'apostates' didn't. (Laughs).

Kurt: Not a single thing. It was a cruel prison.

Natalia: When I felt like I belonged, it was great to feel part of a community. Have loads of great friends all over the country. The social life is the most enjoyable aspect.

Spiral: As an older teenager and 20-something, we had great friends and a good congregation that made you want to be in. Elders were good friends and everyone got along. It was good for awhile! (late 70s early 80s). Then, we ended up in the congo from hell with a brother-in-charge who was (and still is), crazy. That made we wake up.

Eve: I had some real good friends, loved the Bible (still do but read it nowadays much-much less), loved that explanations seemed very logical. We had a foreign language group in the congregation, an English one, of course. I enjoyed reading the books and the Bible in English. I was not too keen on preaching (only if I found genuine interest), but understood and accepted that it was needed.

Marcus: There was nothing that I enjoyed apart from being with friends. Then I discovered they were just 'conditional friends'. Their loss!

Sazzle: I was in a sign language congregation. I learnt to sign really quickly, and have used this skill in my working life. I also learned to be very good at public speaking, another skill I have used in my job.

Gracie: Not applicable.

Mandy: I enjoyed feeling like I had a family that actually cared, and having a lot of support. I enjoyed the fact that everyone was trying to get along. I liked believing there was a god who cared, and that no matter what happened in this life, there was something better to come. I felt safe whilst I believed.

Angus: Identikit friends requiring very little effort.

Robyn: Probably the ready made group of 'friends'. Even though looking back, you know each friendship was entirely false, based on conditional love. At the time, it does feel good to have a lot of friends. But i guess that's what the entire thing is based on, love bombing, the feeling of fellowship and that you're in a great group of people who share your beliefs. That's why they make sure that if you leave, you leave your entire support network behind. Even the friendships are designed to keep people as slaves to the organisation.

Julia: I enjoyed thinking I knew better than everyone else!

Locutus: As a kid, I enjoyed the routine, structure, community. Kids like structure and routine.

Jason: The awesome social life. Meeting different people - not going to lie, the fact that it was easy to chat up girls was a big perk! The assemblies were good, not because of what was being taught but rather, because of being able to meet so many new people.

Paul: I enjoyed knowing that a magic man in the sky was going to make everything better. I would never die, even though my non JW friends were going to be murdered by Jehovah - because he loves you.

Joe: The only thing I can say I truly enjoyed was, when I was young (8-15), I enjoyed feeling as if I knew more about the Bible than the adults I would talk to in the ministry.

Louise: Nothing.

Danmera: I enjoyed being able to rattle off scripture. Thought I knew more than non-JWs. I liked the idea of paradise, getting to meet historical people who have long been dead.

SailAway: I thought I was pleasing God.

Village Idiot: The so-called "knowledge" I was taking in. I remember devouring any book I could get my hands on new or old. I even remember the smell of those books.

Reopened Mind: I enjoyed meeting in small groups for the book study. Afterward we would celebrate couple's anniversaries. So as not to leave out singles and children, we would have a special celebration for them too. I enjoyed visiting other congregations when my husband would give the Sunday talk.

Sue: The long car rides to get to rural territories. The longer the ride, the less time spent knocking on doors!

What is your best/fondest memory?

Flipper: Going to visit my JW mother's NON-JW parents (my non-JW grandparents), at their summer mountain cabin up at a remote lake in the mountains, for a two week vacation each summer, when I was aged 7 to 10 years old. THOSE are some of the happiest memories I have. Fishing with my grandpa, BBQing salmon on their deck at the cabin. The smell of the mountains and mountain air, the trees - those are my happiest memories.

Paula: A friend I made. I still miss her.

Kurt: Secretly laughing at the ignorant things the Elders spoke from the podium.

Natalia: Getting gifts (bribes) from my parents before the assembly. Getting 20p off Dad (more bribes) each time I answered. A meal after a convention with a load of mates, drinking too much and getting a little past tipsy, suggesting the 'Paradise Game' as a joke and found it hilarious when my friends took the game seriously and actually wanted to play.

Spiral: Going skiing and skating with a group of kids. Having costume parties! Feeling like a part of the group. Working food service at the assembly with a bunch of kids. Having fun!

Eve: Trips and cook-outs with friends from the congregation. Cleaning the Kingdom Hall together. Travelling to conventions. Talking about various topics, personal and religious alike, with friends. Singing at the meetings, I liked some songs very much though some not so much. Comparing translations: English, Hungarian and French (I had a friend who was French by birth). I enjoyed book studies where in the small groups people could get to know each other better and there were good conversations after we finished, acts of hospitality, showing genuine love and care.

Marcus: Visiting the city where the convention was. I avoided the sterile and boring sessions. I had to, to keep sane.

Sazzle: Saturday afternoons, after being dragged around bothering the neighbours, going for milkshake and ice cream with my mother and father, before they broke up.

Gracie: Not applicable.

Mandy: I don't have one, in particular. I have lots of memories of doing nice things with nice people. I had a best friend and we went away to Spain together – that was a really good time.

Angus: Parties and BBQ's when I was a child / youth.

Robyn: Couldn't pinpoint just one, but I did have quite a few good times growing up with my friends. We often had sleepovers, midnight snacks, adventurous games, BBQs, camping, activities etc.

Julia: My best memory as a JW, was probably going out for dinner with friends after a long day at a convention!

Locutus: N/A

Jason: Seeing the new Kingdom Hall in local congregation, be erected. It went from the ground to built and carpeted, in the space of 2 days! Was just amazing to see how well organised it was, how quickly it was done - we even had on site catering!

Paul: My best memories are non JW related. Being in the JWs was an austere lifestyle made up of guilt feelings and fear of evil, magical demons. No wonder there is a lot of mental illness within the Watchtower corporation. Assembly dinners. Those segmented trays where the gravy would slop over into the custard compartment. I *really enjoyed* missing meetings. Meetings were drab and depressing. I understand nothing has changed.

Joe: I don't have any fond memories of being a JW, but I do have a few good memories with JW friends.

Louise: Going to Mencap hall as a kid and doing the old time dances. This was because an Elder in our congregation had a mentally handicapped daughter and was involved in the charity Mencap. So we all supported him and went to Mencap Hall for the charity dances.

Danmera: I don't know if it counts as JW related. There was a time when JWs would have "get togethers". One beautiful summer day, we had one of those. Kids playing in the park, good food, etc.

SailAway: Working in food service during assemblies and conventions gave me a sense of belonging and made me feel needed.

Village Idiot: Picnics, playing volleyball, just socializing.

Reopened Mind: For several summers we took our boys camping in the north Georgia mountains. We had time off from our JW routine and were able to bond more as a family. I know that was the only time my Elder husband was able to truly relax. We never went to local meetings during our vacation as the Watchtower suggested.

Sue: Working in food service at a district convention. I felt I was doing something important.

What is your funniest memory?

Flipper: Haven't had a lot of "funny" memories as a JW. Mostly frustrating and sad memories. My funniest memories have been AFTER I exited the JW organization. Just having fun with my son, his girlfriend, and my wife. Lots of fun times playing music, singing, hiking in the mountains - some really fun and funny times.

Paula: Accidentally hitting an Elder's wife with a rounders bat, in the head at the park - HARD!

Kurt: There is nothing funny about being trapped in that cult.

Natalia: An older brother in our congregation walked down the aisle during the service meeting, he coughed, farted really loudly and then followed with an 'ooh!' The back two rows were in stitches and I had to stand out the back because I couldn't stop giggling.

Spiral: Trying to think of something funny (but not tragic), about being a JW..... trying..... trying.....

Eve: As I said, I loved book studies and sometimes the older sisters or brothers told stories from the past, how it was when the witnesses were under ban in our country, how they came together in private homes, how they helped each other, etc. Some of these stories were funny, like this one: One day two brothers were preaching in a cemetery and they saw an elderly woman sitting by a tomb. They went up to her and began to talk about the possibility of resurrection, etc. They also mentioned that in this way she could meet her husband again. The woman exclaimed, Good gracious no! I never want to see him again!

Marcus: The music CD stuttering during one of those turgid kingdom songs. Then, some pious Sister that raised her voice to carry on the song but was singing the words to a different song - this amused me for days. That in itself illustrates the lack lustre life of a JW.

Sazzle: I was at a convention, and bored, so I started drawing. On the convention programme I drew a picture of God, holding the hand of a young Jesus. I wrote a conversation, which went something like, "Pop, what is the meaning of life?" (Jesus). "I will tell you later son" (God). I had also written comments after each speaker had taken their turn. Things like "Crap and sleepworthy", "He looks like he has rubber lips, imagine snogging him, ewhhhhh" etc. Later in the day I realised I had lost my programme and was hunting around for it, when I got a tap on the shoulder and a sister said, "Looking for this?" She had a big smirk on her face and I was mighty relieved – she is now an apostabuddy. (Winks).

Catherine: Being chased by a goose while in field service. The teenage girl in the back seat of my car was laying across the seat laughing at me for how fast I ran.

Gracie: Not applicable.

Mandy: I was in a Sign language congregation so when there were articles about sexual deviancy that had to be signed, it was very graphic – always fun to watch how they chose to sign such parts.

Angus: My wife falling off the platform whilst giving an assignment

Robyn: Aside from getting the giggles during the meeting, or laughing at someone's funny skirt I honestly can't think of any I'm afraid.

Julia: My funniest memory from my days as a JW was the time my Mom rushed out the door to get to the field service group and realized, when she was at the group, that she forgot to put on her skirt! (She had thrown on her long coat over her slip and ran out the door).

Locutus: Giving a talk at ministry school while the crazy Elder's crazy wife breast fed her 6 year old in the front row. My age was 13 at the time. Wow.

Jason: A couple for you - In our old Kingdom Hall, we had to leave the fire door open on hot days as it would get very muggy in there. The brother giving the talk was illustrating Satan being a "bird catcher". With that, a sparrow flew in the fire door and sat on the rostrum! He sat there for ages, poohed on it and then flew away!
A very good friend of mine was reviewing Psalms and read a verse that said, "they all joined in one united throng". However, he said, "one united THONG".

Paul: I put the record player on to a fast speed for the songs, at the Kingdom Hall. Oddly, no one noticed when the songs were really fast.

Joe: When a half-wit was invited to give the closing prayer for the mid-week meeting and at one point said, "we're sorry for all the crap...er..stuff that we do wrong..." Apparently one of the two elderly sisters sitting directly behind me didn't hear what had been said and asked the other for clarification. It was pretty funny hearing an 80+ year old woman say in the most timid voice possible, "he said shit!"

Louise: Being on field service. A man answering the door and saying, "There's a man down there (points down the street), with asbestos teeth, eating cucumbers!" We beat a hasty retreat.

Danmera: I had a part on the platform. Giving a talk. Being a girl, we always had to do those with partners since "women don't teach" from the platform. I was young, what they now call "tween". I got up there, and proceeded to giggle, and giggle, and giggle, and the other girl, a few years older, started to giggle. I never did get to give that talk. It was 2 girls, giggling for 5 minutes.

SailAway: One day out in the field ministry, a much-loved Elder/Pioneer came back to the car stammering, wide-eyed and speechless. A man was out mowing the lawn, and his wife jumped out from behind a bush to surprise him, wearing only a raincoat. She opened the raincoat for the Elder, thinking he was her hubby. The Elder's wife (also a pioneer), was in the car group, and she laughed hysterically. The Elder did not say another word for the rest of the morning.

Village Idiot: I was in school and during recess, I went to a room in the library, where a Sister that I had a crush on, was having a study. As soon as I came in, she said, "Oh, I must put a head covering on," and she lifted her sweater up to her head as an improvised covering. On another occasion, I was out in field service with a Sister (the one I had a crush on), on a very hot day. Someone had the sprinklers on and she, dressed in a skirt, walked right over it with a smile on her face. My most interesting moment was when I and some others, went out in field service, in an isolated part of town. There was this dead goat hanging upside down from a tree, with its throat slit. A little girl, about 5, was yanking the horns back and forth apparently bleeding the animal. The Sister beside me said she was going to throw up but never did. I tried to witness to the people there – they were Spanish speaking – but they kept saying they couldn't understand, even though I was speaking in Spanish. Good for them.

Reopened Mind: When a brother gave a tongue lashing to the congregation for not studying the lesson, until someone informed him had done the wrong one.

Sue: It was one of those long, boring Thursday night meetings. I was already tired from work that day and had to get up early for work the next day, so I just wanted it to end. The Elder chosen to give the last prayer was notorious for droning on and on. There we are, captive audience. Much shuffling of feet to keep awake. At last the final "Amen"! Behind me a little boy says loudly, "About time!" The entire hall heard him and we all laughed. Tell you what, that Elder never gave another prayer on Thursday night.

If you were alive in 1975, as a JW, what do you remember?

Flipper: I remember as a teenager in 1975, Circuit Overseers and speakers from the platform, getting everybody whipped up into an emotional frenzy, claiming that the District and Circuit assemblies would probably be our last in" Satan's wicked system!" That, starting in 1976, we'd very well be having our first assemblies in the "Paradise earth". Those *exact words* were used over the platforms, at Jehovah's Witness congregations and Kingdom Halls. I got whipped up into the frenzy as well. As a young teenager I was spending 102 hours a month, out in service, knocking on doors trying to allegedly, "save people's lives" - but it was all for nought.

It was a lie! Armageddon never happened!

Me, and millions of other people, wasted our lives on a pipe dream. We were ordered by the Watchtower Governing body members, to do so, who knew nothing themselves, they just PRETENDED to know something we did not. So, most of my JW memories are of being "used", or more accurately, "used up" by the Watchtower organization.......

............and lots of wasted years.

Kurt: Just before my time.

Natalia: Not born at this time but have heard a lot about it.

Spiral: I remember thinking it didn't make sense, that it was going to happen in 1975, things didn't seem that bad plus, that's too easy (where's the "comes as a thief in the night" part?). BUT, I do remember hearing it from the platform, at the assemblies - "Stay Alive until 75", and I also remember families who sold everything to pioneer and then suffering financial ruin. Anyone who says it wasn't put out there that 1975 or shortly thereafter would be the end, wasn't there at the time. People absolutely thought that and were encouraged to act on this belief.

Eve: I was not a JW at the time but I remember a sister talking about it, she said it was a trial of faith for the brothers. Many left the religion then but she and her family survived it (she used this verb, well, the Hungarian equivalent).

Marcus: This was a bit before my time. I have seen evidence that the Watchtower did in fact lead the JWs to believe the end would come in 1975. Then, it blamed the false prophecy onto it's followers.

Gracie: I wasn't a JW but I was alive in 1975. The only thing I remember is that JW's did come to the door. My parents hardly ever accepted magazines from them. They basically said they weren't interested and shut the door. I am a Protestant and so are my parents.

I will say, for attending a Protestant church until I turned 17, there was no discussion about other religions/cults. This is where the church I grew up in differs from the Kingdom Hall. As it seems from my visits to the (Ex JW), forum that I learned that all JW's think if you aren't a JW, you are worshipping Satan. I think this was the first real shocking thing I learned. In the eyes of a JW everybody Else's religion is a false religion. In the Protestant church the JW is considered a cult…but nobody thinks they are worshipping Satan.

Mormons, Moonies, Scientology are all thought of as cults. Catholic Church is not thought of as a cult…but more as "they just don't quite have it right." After all, why is there confession? A man isn't responsible for judging you. God is who judges you.

As a kid growing up, attending public schools in Los Angeles - it does seem odd that I didn't have anybody in ANY of my classes who was JW. But, recently there was a video posted by that high school student Brie. I realize now it's very possible I did know a JW….just didn't know I did! I certainly didn't try to find out either. I can tell you right now I never once asked anybody what their religious affiliation was.

I lived in a very Catholic neighborhood. Many of my classmates went to Catechism on Saturdays. They always told me, "you're so lucky you don't have to go." They were right I was super lucky, I wasn't born into any doomsday cult or a religion that required me to do a bunch of things. My religious activities was Wednesday night Bible Study. Sunday morning I had Sunday School followed by the church service. I attended church roughly 3 hours a week. I learned the Bible pretty well during the 4th, 5th, and 6th grade. My mother signed me up for Released Time Classes, which was a class that all you did was, memorize Bible Verses. I won 1st place in that Contest three years in a row. I memorized quite a bit of the Bible between ages 10 to 12. Today I read the Bible but I don't have verses as well memorized. I can find what I need though usually.

I stopped attending church at 17 years old because I decided that I don't need anybody telling me how my relationship with God works. I can pray and read the Bible on my own.

Mandy: I was not a JW at that time.

Angus: I was a kid. My mother was certain '75 would be the year the big A would come. I was worried that I wouldn't make it as I was not the perfect JW school kid. I recall kids mocking us, on the service in '76!

Robyn: Wasn't alive. Although Dad was, and often said that the scandal was because of people getting ahead of themselves and presuming the end was near.

Julia: I was just a baby.

Locutus: I was born in the org in 1964. 3rd generation on my Dad's side, 4th generation on my Mom's. We had no association with worldly people whatsoever, as we had literally thousands of brothers and sisters in the Truth. I grew up in a total "truth" community. I was raised to distrust 'worldly people' and keep 'apart'.

October 1975 was real! I auxiliary pioneered in 1974 at age 10, to try to make the cut. 6000 years of human existence, 7 creative days, and all that mystical math! I can still hear, and remember Fred Franz voice from the convention in 1970, predicting Armageddon in 1975. Grandma used to listen to it on tape again and again as she was a disabled, shut in.

Jason: Not born.

Paul: Yes. I was there. I saw good people give up their homes or get into debt because they thought 1975 was the end. They were looking forward to a loving god slaughtering babies and grown-ups alike, because they weren't Jehovah's witnesses. It WAS stated that Armageddon would arrive in 1975, despite the Watchtower corporation back pedalling on this and blaming everyone else. We only believed what they told us to believe. To doubt them was to doubt the god that was using them as his mouthpiece. In fairness to my Dad (RIP), he didn't hold to the view that 1975 was the end. He just thought it was a 'marked year in Bible history'.

What did I do? I brought a motorbike. 1975 was a filthy trick of the Watchtower corporation to reel in people and thus obtain money and power. Have they (the watchtower corporation), changed? NO! I state here categorically, the Watchtower corporation isn't what you think it is! But, don't take my word for it; do your own research.

Joe: Wasn't alive then.

Louise: I was 5 in 1975 so I vaguely remember it, but not enough to have any critical thinking about it. I remember asking my Aunty Jill about it in 1979 and saying 'wasn't Armageddon supposed to come in 1975' and she got really mad with me and told me off.

Danmera: I was young, but I remember everything. I just remember through the eyes of a kid. I remember the scary talks, the nightmares, the panic. I remember the energy in the kingdom Halls. I remember a lunar eclipse that sent me into a full blown panic attack (although we didn't know that name back then), because the moon was red as blood. I was always on edge, scared, bit my nails till they bled, seriously scary nightmares, the kind that wake you up in a sweat.

When it (Armageddon), didn't happen, the terrifying nightmares faded, mostly went away. I stopped biting my nails. *And*, it planted the first seed of doubt. That seed was planted, but planted deep and took 40 years to break the surface.

SailAway: I remember reading in the Watchtower that I would never be old enough to graduate from college, get married or have children before Armageddon came. I remember the increased pressure and talks from the platform, to do more in the ministry, as the time was short and so many lives were at stake.

There were articles in the Watchtower magazine about the 6,000 years of mankind's existence which helped mark the year 1975. I gave up a college scholarship to pioneer where the need was great, out of high school, as higher education was forbidden. I remember the articles afterward about not serving with a date in view and how some were overzealous. I remember people who went into debt by spending money they didn't have, because they thought they wouldn't have to pay back the loans when Armageddon came. Mostly, I remember nightmares about my family being destroyed at Armageddon and being raped and tortured in a concentration camp for being loyal to Jehovah.

Village Idiot: Yes, definitely. I attended a special talk by Frederick Franz, who was then vice president of the society. It was at the Inglewood Public Forum in Los Angeles. The stadium was packed, maybe 20,000, since there were chairs on the court. I remember having a tape recorder on my lap taping the talk. I wish I had that cassette now. Franz gave a long winded talk which started from creation all the way to the Millennium. In essence he said that the Great Tribulation would start either in 1975 or a few months or years thereafter but not decades. That calculation centered around the "Adam and Eve gap", a period of time between the creation of Adam and Eve which could have been years or decades according to their chronological calculations (keep in mind the "creative days were 7,000 years long). Franz then bizarrely stated that if the Adam and Eve gap were to be decades, Adam would have been tempted into bestiality for lack of a mate. I remember him saying "Would Jehovah allow that? No, Brothers and Sisters."

Reopened Mind: I married in 1974 so I would have someone to go through Armageddon with.

Sue: Mom joined after the 1975 fiasco, but even as a young child I was aware of it. I'd probably heard older JWs talking about it. I do remember asking Mom why didn't Armageddon come like the Society said it would? She told me Jehovah had changed his mind.

Can you think of anything positive to say about the Watchtower organisation?

Flipper: No.

Paula: Excellent at telling lies and cover ups. Could teach the FBI a few things.

Kurt: Not a single thing. The organisation is muck.

Natalia: They're really organised (laughs), and have finally gotten on the technology bandwagon about 10 years later but actually using technology well. Some of the outlines can be interesting, educational and beneficial. Having said that, there are little pieces of good in most religions; you don't have to be a follower to appreciate certain quotes.

Spiral: No, not the org. I know some really nice JWs but there's nothing positive to say about this cult.

Eve: The books and the magazines are of excellent quality, both physically and as to their content, I mean, they can compose their message very well but that does not make it necessarily true of course. They can organize anything very well I think. But this credit may not be due to them, rather, the witnesses themselves, who really believed this was the truth, so sincerely wanted to give their best.

Marcus: No. The whole set up is a heartless machine that will chew you up. Perhaps, yes, if you consider they manage to survive as a scamming big business.

Sazzle: Nothing. I hated being a child in that religion. Whilst some things I enjoyed, like learning sign language – I could have learnt that as a part of normal society without feeling my life had been warped by that fucked up religion.

I remember leaving the religion at 15, and going into a pub at 16. I was expecting to be offered drugs, get beaten up or raped, and for people to be like all those horrible images on the front of the Watchtower. I was shocked to find the experience of being there quite normal.

Catherine: Can't think of anything positive to say.

Gracie: The Awake magazines, if they weren't used to lure people to do harmful things such as shunning, refusing blood transfusions. If they weren't in place for bad reasons. I would say the magazines do have positive things in them. I was reading one that was talking about how to control anger. It's fine to get angry but sometimes it is better to stay positive, depending on the situation of course.

I guess what I am trying to say is, some of the teachings aren't completely destructive. There are some good teachings. There are just too many bad teachings…and the overall idea of having to be so devoted to the man- made organization run by the Governing Body. I am a Christian and as far as I am concerned there is no person on the face of the Earth who can tell me what needs to be done in order to have a relationship with God. I do what needs to be done based upon one basic rule for myself….*"treat others as I want to be treated."*

Mandy: They taught me how to put in to practice some things that would make my life better. The life in the community is good, with lots of support.
I don't regret my time as a JW.

Angus: No.

Robyn: I'm a very confident public speaker because of the training, although I don't know whether that would be the case regardless.

Julia: The children are often polite and well behaved. But it doesn't change the fact that the Watchtower is a cult.

Locutus: Nope. Pure evil.

Jason: Good business people.

Paul: It's a useful community to be a part of. However, the cost is giving your money and soul to gluttonous, greedy, paedophile protecting power trippers in Brooklyn, or wherever they are now, is not worth it. They will take you, break you and once they've bled you dry, they'll spit you out. The Governing body of the JWs are deliberately evil men. All they want is power and your money.

Joe: There's nothing positive about the organization itself. Individual JWs can be quite good people in spite of this, though.

Louise: Nothing.

Danmera: Not anymore. I have pulled back too many curtains, and peeled back too many layers to see anything good anymore. There are still good people inside, but they are good despite the organisation, not because of it. I can no longer see past the corruption, hypocrisy, lies, etc, and what it does to the members and to those who leave, to think of anything good.

SailAway: It served as my substitute family during my pre-teen and teen years and added structure to my life, perhaps saving me from alcoholism and drug addiction, which was the path most of my siblings took.

Village Idiot: Whatever small good they may have is completely tainted by their evil.

Reopened Mind: It gives people structure in their lives who cannot think for themselves.

Sue: When I was young, they seemed like a warm and welcoming family. They steered kids away from drinking and drugs, but I suppose most religious groups and a lot of secular ones do the same.

Do you believe the JWs have the 'truth' or partial truth?

Flipper: No, not at all.

Paula: No.
If 'partially', which 'truth/s' do the JWs have? And this is the question that made me a target. There are at least 4 books missing from the Bible, as we know it. But they don't want to talk about that. (Laughs).

Kurt: No. They twist truth to get money.

Natalia: I think no religion has the truth but there is a little bit of good to be found in most. In terms of other Christian denominations, I feel they are leaps and bounds ahead with the understanding of the Bible from conversations (not ministry!), I have had with friends from other Christian denominations.

Spiral: No way.

Eve: No more than other religions.

Marcus: Never have and never will. The closest they came was saying that religion is a snare and a racket. I didn't realise they were talking about themselves.

Sazzle: No.

Gracie: No, not in any shape or form. I am a Christian and that means that I believe in John 3:16. "For God so loved the world that he gave his only begotten son, that whosoever believeth in him should not perish but have everlasting life."

To me, this means that you are saved - there isn't any of this 'probably' business. The very fact that I read on a forum that the "probably" thing is in existence in the Jehovah's witness - it totally puzzled me. Why?

Why would I want to do something if there's no guarantee? If I was working at a job and my boss said you will "probably" get paid. I would probably quit the next day and get another job. After all I have bills to pay my bills aren't "probably" going to go away!

I think I first read about that 'probably' business in February of this year and I still don't understand that part at all.

I have been reading Steven Hassan's "Combating Cult Mind Control". I haven't finished reading the whole thing. But, it seems to me that people are given promises with guarantees. I haven't finished reading everything yet. I am mostly re-reading a couple of chapters in the middle of the book that discuss ideas to break somebody out of the cult mind control.

This year in January was the very first time I knew that I was talking to someone who was studying with JWs. And it woke me up to the fact that I wasn't neutral. Before, if I heard my friend say that they were planning on getting baptized, I would have just said or I thought I was going to say, well, do what works for you."

I went on-line to see if I was over-reacting about Jehovah's witnesses. And the more I read about them, it just convinced me that I wanted to get involved. And not just with Jehovah's witnesses…but with cult deprogramming in general. I wanted to get involved and educate people BEFORE they sit down and get convinced to join.

In Steven Hassan's book, the one thing I really learned was: "Anybody can be talked into anything at any time!" And you know what…of course we can. It's silly to say we can't. Now if we are forearmed with facts and ask questions. Then of course we can't easily to be talked into anything let alone a cult.

There is one member of my family who is in a cult. My Aunt belongs to Church Universal & Triumphant. My mother says the church used to be here in Southern California and then it moved to Montana. When my Aunt was living in San Diego she was away from family. Her husband at the time (ex-husband), now wasn't a good man. He was attending college, my Aunt paid for him to go. And when he graduated, left her for another woman he got pregnant. The members of the church were super nice to her, and the next thing my family knows, she is a member of this cult. She moved to Montana with the cult. By the time my family knew all of this she was totally indoctrinated. I was in grammar school when all of this happened. My parents didn't tell me she became a member of a cult until I was older. My family did go up to Montana to try and break her out…with absolutely no luck at all. She's this "happy" person, is how I remember my cousin described it when he got back from one of his tries.

Basically my family has given up on even trying to get her out. She is either 79 or 80 now. My mom thinks she was about 30 when she went in. so that's about 40 years she has been in. I know from the fact that my Aunt is in a cult…that we can be talked into anything at any time! If we don't know beforehand that it's harmful!

I threw a party for my mom's 65th birthday. I offered to send my Aunt a ticket to come to the party. She wouldn't come. The party was the week of their Conventions. I told her all the rest of her brothers and sisters were coming. I wanted to get a picture of all the brothers and sisters together while we still could. She still wouldn't even fly out for the day…I offered to pay for everything. A taxi/rental car..or airfare. Anything to get her here. I even told her I would buy her a new outfit if that was an issue. Anyway, nothing I said worked. Do I ever plan to go to Montana to visit her? I don't know if I can handle that. Now that I know how destructive cults work, I think it would just be a circular conversation. But, of course last year I would have said...oh well, JW's just think differently than me. Basically my Aunt didn't come because she needed to be there for what they call "Open House." But, really it's their recruiting week.

Today, I say they are a doomsday cult. I am talking to every single person I know to make sure they understand what a destructive cult is. My goal is to make sure I never, ever hear someone say "I am joining "name a cult," ever again!

If 'partially', which 'truth/s' do the JWs have? There is no partially to the truth. I am a Christian, you either have the truth or you don't. Someone told me I sounded just like a JW when I said that last statement. (Laughs).

I said that's an insult if you don't know. Why? Well...for starters, I don't think everybody worships Satan. I also celebrate my birthday 31 days out of the month, Christmas....and even though these things may not seem important. It is important because it shows that I don't think like a JW does. I believe in free will for all. I believe you have the right to decide whether or not to believe in God. I have no interest in trying to change any one's mind. But, if someone is looking, and wants to talk about beliefs, I am willing to discuss the Bible with anyone. But, I wouldn't knock on someone's door to do so...as a JW would.

Mandy: No. I don't believe any religion has.

Angus: No.

Robyn: Hell No!

Julia: Absolutely not!

Locutus: Nope.

If 'partially', which 'truth/s' do the JWs have? They believe the earth is round. We agree on this point.

Jason: NO!

Paul: Never in a million years!

Truth is not a commodity. It cannot be owned by some paedophile protecting men in America, let alone anyone else. Truth simply exists. Something is either true or it isn't.

Jehovah's witnesses use the term 'truth' without realising it's a mind control technique. (Look the subject up). They say, "I'm in the truth," or "He has gone out of the truth." What poppycock!

So. In answer to the question and without laughing in derision, my answer is a resounding: 'NO!'

They never did speak truth and probably never will.

My alternative answer is, HAHAHAHAHAHAHAHAHAHAHAHA!

Joe: Absolutely not.

Louise: No. None. None whatsoever.

Danmera: No.

SailAway: Absolutely not!

Village Idiot: Yes (Laughs). No. Absolutely not. Not even close.

Reopened Mind: No.

Sue: Hell, no!

Would you recommend being a JW and why do you answer thus?

Flipper: No, I do NOT recommend that anybody becomes a JW at all. Run for your life from this high control organization. You will lose your freedom of mind to a mind control cult that will suck all the emotional, mental, and physical energy you have left in your body. It will suck away the time you have in your life, to do the bidding of WT leaders, so they can sustain their Billion $$$$ organization for their own financial betterment.

Meanwhile; your financial betterment becomes non-existent as you donate time, money, effort into a huge organization that really, doesn't care about your welfare. YOU as a person - really do NOT matter. What matters to Watchtower leaders is the advancement of Watchtower organizational interests - not individual interests. So if you cherish your freedom of mind do NOT join this organization.

Paula: NEVER. Cult mentality that destroys families in the name of a 'loving God'. Bullsh1t. If Jah can talk to the Elders, but not 'us', then one of us is mentally ill. A$$holes.

Kurt: Suicide is a better option than joining that insane cult. Perhaps they will insist the followers kill themselves after leaving everything in their will to the organisation.

Natalia: I think if you are maybe lonely or looking to quench your spirituality and don't mind not thinking for yourself, go for it. There are a lot of nice and well-meaning people and being part of a community feels great. Personally, I don't think you need to be a JW or follow any other religion to lead a satisfying and God-pleasing (if you believe) life. I wouldn't encourage anyone in life one way or another. Whatever makes one happy.

Spiral: No, don't drag that bunch of trouble into your life.

Eve: I would not. It had a certain role in my life but it basically robs people of their conscience. If someone obeys the advice coming from the magazines (the Governing Body), instead of their own conscience, it is a very dangerous thing in my view (if the two are at odds). This religion couldn't rob me of my conscience because I did not let it do it.

Many times I was admonished to do more in the ministry or to obey the advice given to me. E.g. There were a couple of months when because of dental problems, I was not willing to comment on the meetings. Elders and others encouraged me to do that nevertheless, saying it did not matter to them. But I was adamant, it did matter to me and I didn't care what they thought, though of course, I did not say so. Because of such things, I was not an exemplary witness but neither was I someone they had serious problems with. I attended the meetings and did my share in the ministry, but there were certain things that I did not let them interfere with, like what music I listen to, what books I read or how I raise my children. I never let this religion come between my children and me. Some sisters considered themselves first of all, their children's 'Bible teacher' and only secondly their mother. I did not, even though I got an advice to do that. So when my children told me they would not want to go on studying, I did not press them about it, even though I was sad, because I felt it was the truth at the time and that it was my duty to convey that kind of thinking and way of life towards them. But, after a while my conscience stopped me somehow and I listened to it. Luckily, none of them became a witness, probably just because of that.

Now I can see this religion for what it really is, but this doesn't mean that I feel those years were wasted. When I became a witness, it seemed to me the best decision and I would do the same if I knew only the information I knew at that time. But of course if I had known then all the things I know now, I would never have dreamed of becoming a witness. It happened like this and I believe it was meant to happen for some reason. And I was meant to leave when the time came for that. That's that. Smiles.

Marcus: Steer well clear of this lot, for your own sanity. The leaders just want your money and possessions. They are legalised thieves.

Sazzle: No, I hope I live to see the whole religion crumble. I grew up believing all those awful Armageddon stories, and seeing my parents reacting every time there was a news story about an earthquake or flood. They were almost rubbing their hands with glee that it proved Armageddon was close.

I wasn't allowed to choose my own friends. I wasn't allowed to celebrate anything that everybody else celebrated. I had to do my school work and study for the meetings, and spend every Saturday morning traipsing round after my parents, and feeling embarrassed when they knocked on a door to find a school friend at that house.

I was home schooled from 11 years old, so became more isolated, and had no real friends in the congregation, so became very lonely. Then when I decided to leave at 15 years old, had so much hassle from my parents and the Elders. I am really glad I never got baptised. My sister did and my parents won't speak to her. At least I am allowed to speak to them. I think it is one crazy f**ked up religion.

Gracie: Before January of 2015 I would have said, or at least I thought I would have said....whatever works for you. My parents raised me to respect other people's beliefs. And even though they did classify Jehovah's witness as a cult...surprisingly enough, it took my friend to start studying with the Jehovah's witnesses for them to actually say out loud..."that's a cult!."

I have to say when I first heard them say that...I mean here I am 47 years old. And even though Mormons, Jehovah's Witnesses...and some other groups came to the door. My parents just said we aren't interested. Shut the door...and that was it. Maybe on a rare occasion they would say...they believe in some far out things. I never bothered asking what. Since they didn't make a big deal about it...it didn't peak any curiosity at all!

My main reasons for not wanting anybody to become a JW:
1. Judicial committee
2. There is the secret Elder's book
3. The deceitful way they recruit new Studies.
4. Not being able to celebrate holidays.
5. Refusing blood transfusions
6. Two-witness rule...and apparently the three witness rule if you want to accuse an Elder.
7. Door to door witnessing.....you can't earn your salvation. It's faith.
8. Baptism..... You don't get into heaven by being baptized. Your faith is all that matters. After all was the thief who was crucified at the same time as Jesus baptized? Probably not.
9. Not planning for the future. (not saving money because you think Armageddon is coming is a bad piece of advice....of course this is because the Watchtower wants all the money.)
10. Takes away your ability to be human. (Happy, happy happy all the time?? In order to truly appreciate being happy we have to experience some days of sadness. This philosophy is only encouraging mental problems.)
11. The biggest reason of all. It destroys families with its shunning practices! (A true Christian doesn't shun, they try to show love towards everyone.)

Mandy: No, I would not recommend it, because it is not the truth.
I found life as a JW comfortable, supportive and I felt safe. I felt safe amongst a community of people who helped me, and with the thought that whatever went wrong, paradise was coming. But I realised it was not the truth. When you do, no matter how comfortable the life, you cannot go on living a lie. You shall know the truth and the truth shall set you free - ironically, words that are attributed to Jesus Christ; I do believe that however hard life is, it is better to live in truth than fool yourself with a lie.

Angus: Absolutely not!

It is a controlling cult led by morally reprehensible, self-serving hypocrites who don't care about the safety of its membership. The main focus of the cult is to fleece its members of their money, dignity and self-esteem.

JW's have their humanity slowly sucked out of them until they are no more than zombies, manipulated and controlled by their evil, slave-driving masters.

Robyn: No comment made.

Julia: Absolutely not!

The Watchtower is a cult and I feel very sorry for anyone that has fallen under its control.

Locutus: The JW organization promotes simplistic thinking, denies it's members education, and discourages personal achievement. It prefers to keep it's people child like, controllable, and simple minded. It promotes magical thinking, rather than rational thinking. Members typically are simple and uneducated, and most often have a victim mentality. The "no part of this world" teaching divides people along religious divides, and justifies lack of motivation or ambition as a virtue.

Jason: No!

They take away this amazing thing called life! You can't make ANY decisions at all, from what film you can watch, to what position you can have sex with your wife, in the bedroom.

Not only that, but if you believe in God like I do, they make him feel so far away and make you jump through so many hoops to get to him.

If I am being honest, I know that for 23 years all I was, was a watchtower puppet – saying and doing everything they told me.

They take away your freedom, your family, your friends, your career, your money, your time, your life. In return they give you a social life and a small chance of living forever in paradise, but only if your good enough.

Paul: Do you want to be prevented from celebrating Birthdays, Christmas and other celebrations and be told that if you do celebrate, God will kill you soon?

Do you want loved ones to die because men in Brooklyn say you are not allowed a lifesaving Blood Transfusion?

Do you want to belong to a religion that makes numerous false prophecies about the end of the world?

Do you want to belong to a religion that hides the identities of paedophiles, won't report them to the authorities and allows them to still associate with your children?

Do you want to have ALL your thoughts controlled by men in the U.S.A?

If you answered 'YES' to these questions, then you should join Jehovah's Witnesses.

WARNING: Please check the Sex Offenders Register before allowing a Jehovah's Witness into your home.

Joe: I would recommend strongly *against* becoming a JW. This is not a religion as such; it is a cult that offers no benefit that cannot be found elsewhere in a much healthier way. It is a system designed to put people in a mental prison and enslave them to a corporation run by what must either be, half-wits or completely morally bankrupt men.

Louise: I would recommend someone become a follower of the Wombles before they join the JWs. At least The Wombles cleaned up the litter in Wimbledon Common, in a fictional cartoon.

Danmera: I would NOT recommend anyone being a JW, any more than I would recommend someone being part of Jonestown, or Scientology, or ISIS, or any other mind control organisation. I can no longer see it as a benign "religion". It's harmful and destructive hiding behind clean and smiling people.

SailAway: I would in no way recommend becoming a JW.

The organization is a destructive, high control group (cult), that destroys human potential by forbidding higher education. It destroys families by its disfellowshipping doctrine and mandatory shunning. It puts lives at risk due to the ban on blood transfusions. It protects pedophiles by implementing the "two-witness rule" and treating child molestation as a sin to be handled by the congregation Elders, rather than a crime that needs to be reported to, and handled by the proper authorities. The organization lies to its members and prints revisionist history to cover its tracks.

Village Idiot: Are you joking? I'd rather die than to live a living death. There is nothing that religion has to offer.

Sue: I would tell everyone to stay far away from this group. It is toxic, especially for vulnerable children. I spent many sleepless nights as a kid terrified that Jehovah would kill me for some 'sin'. I was raised to distrust non-JWs since they weren't really good people. Even if they seemed nice, Satan was just using them to lure us away from the 'truth'. I was constantly anxious that I would do something 'wrong' and God would hate me. I was always feeling guilty for doubting what I was being told. I felt humiliated every time I couldn't take part in school holiday activities and had to leave the room. I struggle with low self-esteem, having grown up bombarded by literature asking 'Are you doing enough?' and 'Could you be doing more?' The not-so-subtle message was that I was NOT doing enough for the Society and should do more, no matter how I felt or what I wanted. I'm still a people pleaser, desperate for the approval of others and anxious when I don't get it. Worst of all, I grew up having to be secretive. From a young age I knew I couldn't be honest and say what I really thought about the Society; my best friends and family would turn me in and then they would shun me. Now in my married life I find myself holding back my true thoughts and feelings, afraid my husband will reject me.

All those things led me to begin 'fading' as a JW starting around the age of 18. I still hung around the edges as it were, going to meetings once in a while, but otherwise inactive. I was 25 when I went to a district convention with my JW family. There I heard one of the speakers in his talk explaining why JWs shouldn't give to charities: because Jehovah was going to kill all those people at Armageddon anyway, so the money would be wasted. I felt like someone had kicked me wide awake. I looked around, wondering why everyone else wasn't as shocked as I was, but they were just sitting there smiling. That callous statement slapped me across the face and made me realize I couldn't be part of this religion any longer. I went out to the car at lunch and sat there the rest of the day. I haven't set foot in a Kingdom Hall since, except for my baby sister's wedding.

Please tell us what *you want us to know* about being a JW.

Flipper: As a JW you will NOT be told the total truth about what's going on in a criminal way within the WT organization. ***Criminal child abuse is being covered up***. People have been Disfellowshipped for telling the truth about existing pedophiles among Jehovah's Witnesses. According to court documents there are 23,000 known JW pedophiles right now, in the

Watchtower Society database in their own computers, that they know about. Watchtower Society REFUSED to hand over this information at the order of the courts, costing them 13.5 million $$$$ due to the 'standing in contempt of court'. (Bet you weren't told this at your local Service meeting announcements).

People have died due to following the Watchtower Society leaders instructions about not receiving blood transfusions. Watchtower Society continues to request money and financial support from poorer JW's, so as to finance the "worldwide witnessing work" – which, when translated, is really financing the "Watchtower Society property and real estate land grab work".

So that's it. Watchtower Society is a real estate marketing company disguised as a religion, intent on furthering it's Billion $$$ empire at the expense of the widow's mite, the poorer JW's. It entraps the minds and freedoms that people once had before they join this mind control cult. Watchtower Society is a criminal organization, with criminal intent, all done with a smile on the face of Stephen Lett, on JW.org T.V.

Run people, run away from this!

Paula: Brainwashing is real, even when you're a member of MENSA, and have a degree in brain surgery - IRONIC!!

I had moved back to my 'homeland' after 17 years in Coventry. I was ill - agoraphobia, anxiety, panics - in short - a mess. Lost my job as a nurse, all friends, income - had no friends so life was tough. Hell.

Then my best friend who lived in Watford, died in a car crash, while 6 months pregnant. I hit rock bottom. I could only sit in the garden for short periods of time and became housebound.

Three months on from the death of my darling friend, there was a tap at the door. Two 'pretty' young girls stood there. I suppose they were around 20 - 25. They explained who they were and I was happy to chat.

Thus began an informal 'pop in to see how you are' - AKA 'LOVE BOMBING'.

They were kind and helpful, concerned and 'worried' about me. To be told that 'Jah' loved me anyway, despite my ill health, was wonderful as I could still be useful. Little did I know, but these 'loving sisters' would eventually turn my illness against me by insinuating I wasn't praying hard enough and my agoraphobia was no excuse for not going on the ministry.

...and about this time, my husband left me.

I began a regular study and attended the Kingdom Hall for about 2 years, sitting at the back. Panic! They told me I was safe there.

Then began the difficult issues of Christmas, blood, birthdays, sex in marriage, idols etc....and slowly and surely they drew their plans against us (sorry), took over my thinking as I was eager to comply. I began to take my son aged 6-7, to the Kingdom Hall. I even persuaded my husband to attend the 'Memorial' twice.

In December 2008, my son had a laptop as a present (not from me, as I didn't care about X-mas), as he needed it to complete school work. By this time I had broken and disposed of all my Rock CDs. (Around 50!).

I got rid of the gold and diamond cross that my husband had brought me for our wedding day. Thrown out letters, cards and presents from a good friend as she was a 'pagan'. That hurt!

I signed a 'no blood directive'. I wrote to a local church to have my name removed from the Christening register. I only wore skirts and got rid of almost all of my 'worldly' clothes. I was praying before all meals - tea towel on my head. I only associated with JWs. My anxiety was not better. I became suspicious of anyone not a JW! Anxiety no better, I spent hours alone studying and praying, crying and pleading. Was making plans for my 'baptism', if only I could just 'get over' this agoraphobia and anxiety - surly it was all in my head?!!??! I must try harder but couldn't understand what I was doing wrong.

I learned to use the laptop quickly but was very vigilant in avoiding 'apostate' sites. Then one day, instead of finding my 'favourites' list, I opened a new tab and typed in 'JW'......................JW.Net popped up. The rest, as they say, is history. Thank God (Laughs).

I began to question doctrine and became known as 'a bit of a worry'. Where had the compliant me gone?

Soon, Elders came. Then I was stopped from arranging the flowers for funerals and the Kingdom Hall in general. That had been my only outlet.

I could see people whispering about me. I became paranoid but could not escape the feeling that something was very wrong. Just hang in there - that would help me.

My friendships on the website developed quickly. The stories I read I devoured. I learned to research and develop critical thinking. This takes us up to March 2009. By now I had almost stopped attending the Kingdom Hall. Elders called again. The memorial wasn't far off and I was told, "you are either *for* Jehovah or *against* him!"

I was told this was the 'truth', 'accept it or not' but now was the time for a decision on my part. I decided I would go ahead with baptism after the memorial, as that would cause me panic with crowds. I stopped posting on the website. Then something incredible happened that changed everything. My mothers' death saved my life.

She was admitted for a routine bowel operation. I was already in constant anxiety as the memorial in Cardiff was only 3 days away. My mother survived the operation - the relief was immense. She had COPD, asthma and bronchitis. I went to the Kingdom Hall and told my 2 buddies, surely, this was a sign from Jah!

One day from the memorial and the hospital called all the family in. The surgeon had nicked my Mam's bowel and she had developed septicemia. She was in intensive care and was going to die.

I stayed with her all night. Returning home I quickly dressed, hurried to the Millennium Stadium. I was an hour late, but was sure it was okay, my friends would understand......wouldn't they?

Time broke down into a series of crystal clear moments as I entered. Disapproving looks - whispers. I stumbled to my seat, overwhelmed by the noise (speakers), lights, crowds -

I found my 'best friend' - as I collapsed into my seat, the first words out of her mouth were, "you're late!"

I explained my mother was in intensive care and doctors were going to plan to turn off her life support in 2 days time. I was met with a blank stare. You know, the 'dead behind the eyes' look. Like a shark.

I sat and endured the wonderful 'new light' and 'spiritual food at the proper time' for around 30 minutes. I was sweating and fighting off the urge to run away. My heart pumped like an engine and I lost sensation in my face and my eyes became blurry.

Suddenly - and quite unexpectedly, a sense of calm came over me along with the thought 'you should be with your Mam!'

I got up and looked at all my 'friends' as I left. I went to the hospital and spent an hour with my Mam. I talked to her. I washed her. I arranged her hair. I remember thinking how beautiful her skin looked as I held her hand.

My brother switched off the machine at 3:50pm the next day. I never went back to the Kingdom Hall.

I had just 2 visitors in the weeks that followed. Shortly afterwards, I wrote a letter to the Elders and posted it directly through the Kingdom Hall door. Angus and Jane visited me a month later.

Then I was FREE!

Kurt: This is not a religion. It is a soul destroying, life destroying cult of evil.

Natalia: If the truth sets people free - why does being a JW feel so claustrophobic and like you are prisoner?

Being a JW can feel good at times (Stockholm Syndrome?); knowing so many people and having so many friends. Any friendship formed, however, is conditional. Should you decide there are things you don't believe in or agree with or things you don't want to do, you'll find yourself without friends because you are a 'bad association' and have 'apostate thinking'. Not celebrating holidays isn't such an issue (for me) - they are expensive! And have never really bothered me anyway, but for some, it's a much bigger thing.

As a child/teen; it can be very difficult being the odd one out at school. Not allowed to hang around with your 'worldy' friends can make you feel isolated if you have no Witness friends. This can be really damaging to a child/teen's development. I would say it damaged me. I wanted to go to university, take part in the Duke of Edinburgh award scheme and do sports after school but I wasn't allowed. I convinced myself that it was because I wanted to do everything for 'Jehovah', but really I was just softening the disappointment I was feeling at my parents saying no. I was too scared to even kiss a boy!

Having a boyfriend was a big no-no. You don't learn how to grow up properly. You don't get to make any mistakes and learn from them. I feel like my life has regressed - in my 20s, I'm doing all the things I didn't do as a teenager!

Jehovah's Witnesses claim they have an answer to all questions. When I was a child, I remember asking my parents how people know they are anointed.

The answer I received was that, at their baptism, 'they just know'. That didn't make too much sense to me, but I accepted it. Later I learnt that it is people who do not have an 'earthly hope' and it all just seemed a little ridiculous, especially as the only anointed members I have ever met have actually been deemed as mental by others! But you accept things without question because that is how you are taught. For me, this adversely affected my life as I would not challenge anything, not just Jehovah's Witness related but at school or at work for example; I would often concede when authoritative figures demanded (although not to the detriment of 'Jehovah' of course).

A lot of people today are so apologetic, I think that being a Jehovah's Witness you will be an apologist. You say sorry for everything and even things that you don't have to be sorry for. This is mentally unhealthy and reduces self-esteem. I have finally stopped saying sorry for ridiculous little things I am not actually sorry for; if I am not sorry, I will not say it. It has not made me an arrogant or egotistical person, more self-aware and confident.

Ultimately, there is both good and bad with being a Jehovah's Witness, but I really think it depends how awake you are.

Spiral: If you feel you want to have a spiritual part to your life (however you define that), please don't think that JWs are the way to go. They are a depressed bunch of people. Everyone I know who's been in for years (mid-life plus), is just sad and depressed, struggling along. The org makes them that way! They are just waiting to start living their life in the new order and some are barely making it (in all respects), in their daily life. And now they are afraid to really figure out what they need. So sad!

Eve: One thing is sure, you cannot speak about all of them under the same breath. They are just as different as any other persons.

Marcus: I want you all to know that the JWs are trained liars and they don't en know it. They will ease you in with honeyed words and false promises. Once you're in, they will treat you as a slave. The leaders will guilt trip you into giving them your money and possessions.

Ask any JW and they will deny it all. Secretly, they know it's true but dare not admit it to themselves because once they're out they'll be shunned. They stand to lose everything including family.

Abandon hope, all ye that enter. It's a big business, a cult. The leaders only want power, money and a rock star lifestyle and they don't care if you suffer and die, as long as they get it.

Sazzle: Being a Jehovah's Witness means you sign your soul over to the Organisation. Everything you do is judged. Every decision you make will be based on, "Will it make Jehovah happy?"

You will have to put the religion first, even above close family members. If a close family member is disfellowshipped or disassociated, you have to stop all contact with them, so they don't influence you badly.

Everything you do is scrutinised. If you skirt is too short, your ear rings too big, your dress too strappy, your attitude unchristian, you drink one too many beers, you watch something "worldly" on the TV, etc etc., you can be called to account. It really felt for me, like those who got baptised, had sold their right to have their own view – in fact thinking for yourself is not a Christian quality.

The Watchtower tells you how to think, and you must obey. The religion sucks. I will be glad to see its downfall. I believe it will come one day : I hope it is in my day.

Gracie: If you are "a never was a Jehovah's witness" as I am, and you are reading this and you think that it doesn't matter that someone is joining a cult.

Ponder this question:
Your great grandchild answers the door and it's a Jehovah's witness that says "Would you like to study the Bible?"
And your great grandchild says, "yes."
"How would that make you feel?"

Or, worse yet, your spouse, who has been home because they are sick, while you are working on the job, says to you "I have been studying with Jehovah's witnesses and about to be baptized."

It happens!

Studies are encouraged to keep the fact they are studying a secret.

So, yes, have the conversation with everybody, at least once, about religions/cults. Otherwise someone you love could land in a doomsday cult.
I wish and I always will wish, for the rest of my life, that I had even ONE conversation with my friend who is studying with the JW's, BEFORE she told me she was studying.

Now I am making sure I have that one conversation with everybody. I don't want anybody to have to go through what I am currently going through. It's tough watching the cult-like traits take over my friend. And that's basically what I want to say.

Mandy: When you do the home bible study it all makes sense; the scriptures match everything you are taught. But this is a superficial level. When you start learning from other books like Revelation, Daniel, etc., it is pretty obvious to anyone using their brain – that the explanations given by the org make no sense; they are just trying to make it 'fit' their belief system.

I left when I saw a 12 year old girl baptised. Baptism for a JW means a serious vow to Jehovah God, to serve him forever. It's "more serious than marriage" I was told. To get baptised the candidate has to meet with the Elders and answer questions, so their suitability for baptism can be established. The Elders then decide if someone is ready for baptism.

I questioned the Elders about why they would allow a 12 year old to be baptised, and was told I was displaying unspiritual and apostate thinking. Yet my reasoning was logical. A 12 year old is a minor and cannot sign any legal contract. Yet, they can be baptised into an organisation that takes their vow so serious, should they decide later they don't want to be a jw and leave, they can end up shunned by an entire community. For many young people, they have grown up in that religion. Every human they care about belongs to that organisation. When they become mature enough to decide their baptism was done when they were too young to understand the implications, and want to leave; they lose everything they have ever known. In my view it is the Elders who allowed a child baptism who should be shunned and ostracized. It was seeing this unfairness; that made me leave, and never want to go back.

Angus: As a child, being a JW destroys any potential you have to make a meaningful contribution to society. It destroys your self-esteem and ability to think. You never mature into a free thinking adult, you are left dependent on the mother organisation and your decisions are based on their edicts.

The Watchtower society is pure poison.

Robyn: I guess I'd like everyone to know that being a JW is extremely damaging, it
ruins families, and ruins lives.

Those that do manage to escape, often go on to struggle with many aspects of the outside world, trying to return to normality.

Being a JW is like living in a big bubble, where you are happy to deny the nose on your face if it keeps up the charade. You live in fear of constant impending doom. You feel daily guilt as you are reminded that you are solely responsible for saving people from gods killing spree. Success is measured in literature distributed.

Julia: Jehovah's Witnesses appeal to people that want answers but sometimes the answer is, 'there is no answer'. I am learning every day how to be okay with that!

Locutus: Been there. Done that.

Jason: I want you to know that 90% of the JW's I know where lovely people. They have been tricked in to believing the Watchtower is a godly organisation. I fully admit I was tricked and then what is even cleverer, is that you are forbidden of reading ANYTHING critical about the Watchtower. Therefore, you only ever see one side of the argument.

Most people will say being a JW is great. That's because they have never known what it's like *not* to be one, and to be 100% sure that it is a false religion.

Paul: The Watchtower corporation will bleed you dry and send you insane. They will ease you into their religion with love bombing and seeming answers to life's problems. You will be told lies about your freedom to leave. Once you are baptised, you will then find out the real face of this high control cult. Then, you are trapped.

Joe: It's a harmful cult that has cost more lives than Heaven's gate, Jonestown, and the Branch Davidians combined.

Louise: Nothing.

Danmera: It's all an illusion. As long as you stay in lockstep, think what they want you to think, say what they want you to say, act how they want you to act, etc, you can believe you are happy, or that you are in "the truth". Really look at their "hope", their version of paradise is really selfish. They will do anything, step on anyone, hurt, shame, guilt, shun etc, just so they get theirs.

They also have to spend "eternity" under the gun, one misstep and zap, they can lose it all.

Don't be fooled by a pretty picture, or what you may see as "nice people", and all the pulls on your emotions. It's all very slick, and if you aren't careful, it can pull you in. Most are only "nice" when they feel they can convert you. As soon as it's clear they cannot, you will more times than not, see a totally different side of them. Any company that says, 'listen only to us only, go to OUR site...only read what we print....and that everyone else is a liar'...should send up red flags. One should be allowed to listen to reviews from previous owners.

SailAway: I suffered a life time of severe clinical depression, generalized anxiety disorder and Post-Traumatic Stress Disorder as a JW, in large part due to the doctrines, beliefs and practices of the organization. Cognitive dissonance nearly killed me. Mishandling of a personal crisis in my son's life by the Elders nearly killed him. He is now disfellowshipped, and I was expected to shun him. That just wasn't going to happen.
I have been out for nearly four years now and am medication free and happy. The organization interferes in marriages and family lives with all of its rules and heavy demands on time and resources. It isolates people with the Us vs.Them mentality that "worldly people" (including non-believing family members), are under Satan's control and wicked. My immediate family is all out of the organization, and we have mended the rifts caused by the organization. My in-laws are still in and have continued to shun their only son, my husband, for over 30 years. They now shun me and our children as well and have no interest in getting to know their first great grandchild—all because we left the organization.

Village Idiot: Nothing but grief. If you're reading this and you're new to the Witnesses please, PLEASE run away as fast as you can!

Reopened Mind: If you want an organization to intrude into every aspect of your life, then being a JW is for you. But if you want to make your own decisions and be free create your own life, then stay as far away from this cult.

Sue: When you become a JW, you sign away your intellectual freedom. If you are a JW, you must NEVER openly question what you're taught. You must NEVER admit to having doubts. If you do and the Elders can't make you recant, you WILL be 'disfellowshipped': shunned. Your best friends, even you closest family, will be expected to treat you as if you don't exist: to walk past you on the street as if they don't see you; to not even smile at you in greeting. The goal is to make you miserable and force you back into the fold. Think very carefully before you decide study with JWs. They will seek to control every aspect of your life.

Some extra comments

Paula

What made you leave? Internet knowledge. The JWs wanted me to choose between them and my family. My dead mother won.

Is your life better? 100% - I have my life back, my dignity, critical thinking skills, real friends who love me despite my problems.

My poor hubby and son. But hubby never stopped me, so I carried on I guess.

Bill S

What made you leave? For me initially, it was what an archaeologist friend of mine called 'inconvenient dates'. I studied with her for a while when I was in. She hooked onto the theory that Adam and Eve had only been on this Earth for 6000 years, and commenting on utensils she has held in her hands that were 18,000 years old, which were obviously man made. I half heartedly responded with, "well, the materials were maybe that old but after looking into it, seems the science is right."

I know the Earth itself is billions of years old, as the account of creation uses days as an unspecified length of time, not a 24 hour day as we know it. But it was this fact that people had been on the Earth for longer than 6000 years that blew my mind. Started thinking then.

After that, it was the way my step son's Judicial committee was handled, and actions of certain Elders (that shouldn't have been Elders), and some of the congregation, that just said to me, 'I don't belong here any more.'

Is your life better? That was nearly 10 years ago now. My life is ace. Got a beautiful woman, a nice house, a good dog, good friends, a good relationship with my Mum and Dad, who are still in and my sister, who is making roads back in, but half heartedly - And as the rock band Thunder said, "I'm a better man for it."

Kurt: I saw the evil and darkness in the cult. It was unbearable. If I had not left, I would have killed myself. When I left I felt such great relief.

Sue

What made you leave? I've already mentioned the straw that broke this camel's back: the callous attitude of JWs toward charities. But that was just the climax to years of doubts and frustrations building up. I'd always had an interest in archaeology and ancient history so, I knew scientific evidence was lacking for Bible stories. I also have an interest in medical topics so I knew there was no valid reason for refusing blood transfusions; it was just a rule made up by men with no knowledge of medicine. The idea that JWs shouldn't give to charity because God was going to kill everyone anyway and it would be wasted effort was what really did it, though. I could NOT stay in a religion that encouraged such a cold-hearted attitude to fellow humans.

What did you do different? I became a registered voter. I donated blood for the first time. I read 'apostate' literature and surfed the Internet and the results were eye-opening! I give to charities. One year, I had a blast volunteering at a Halloween trick-or-treating event my employer was part of. I began to date a 'worldly' man (over my JW mother's loud objections!), and now we've been married for almost eight years. I read whatever I want, watch whatever I want, and talk to whoever I want.

Am I happier?

Yes. A huge weight lifted off me when I left the Kingdom Hall for the last time. I no longer feel pressured to spend all my time trying to meet the Society's impossible goals. Best of all, I'm not afraid of doing something 'bad' and having God butcher me and eight billion other people at Armageddon. My JW family could always choose to shun me, but that was something I accepted might happen when I began to fade. That chance is a bit of a cloud in my life, but I don't dwell on it. I can't live that lie anymore and I hope my family at least respects that I'm trying to live my life honestly.

Russ
What made you leave? Just couldn't accept that Armageddon was imminent, and got fed up of battling to convince myself that it was true - there just wasn't enough evidence to back it up.

What did you do differently? Started thinking critically. Became a sceptic. Made friends with 'worldly' people. Wrote a couple of books. Did a charity skydive. Gave blood. Voted. Made beer. Watched motorcycle racing. Drew pictures. Stuff I didn't have time for before.

Is your life better? In most ways, yes. My JW family members won't talk to me, which I find annoying and offensive, but I don't really miss their company. As my wife is still a JW, there are times when family life is more difficult now, but not often. I would much rather live with a free mind and the ability to learn new things without having to filter them through Watchtower beliefs first, than live the semi-comatose life of a JW. And I sure as hell don't miss going to meetings or on the ministry!

Paul

What made you leave? Over the years, things didn't add up. When I was an Elder and part of a judicial committee, there was something that puzzled me.

As Elders, we would give god's supposed judgement on a matter. It was supposed to be from holy spirit direction. Then why was the 'wrongdoer' given 7 days to appeal the decision? Surely, if it was a decision from God, there was no question about it.

Finally, in 2010, the Watchtower corporation brought out the new light of overlapping generations. I saw this as them just covering their backs because Armageddon had failed to arrive. This was despite what they had written, but later denied or altered in their books.

I had to leave - sanity demanded it.

What did you do differently? I went to a church to worship. I later became an atheist.

I helped out in a soup kitchen. I became a much kinder person despite the unchristian shunning from JWs.

Is your life better? No. My life is awful. The family broke up as a result. Despite the Watchtower corporation claiming they don't break up families - they most certainly do - they are liars. They actively promote with menaces, the shunning of family if a family member decides to leave the corporation. A Watchtower corporation spokesman lied to the press. He said that shunning was an individual choice. Every JW knows that if they talk to a shunned person they themselves will be kicked out and shunned. The Watchtower corporation is merciless, heartless and disingenuous on an enormous level. They keep it hidden from the public. **Never trust what Watchtower corporation claims!**

However, I am true to myself and not living a lie.

Catherine

What made you leave? I had experienced over my thirty years in, of feeling like it was just a numbers game, counting hours, the more you get, the better treated you are. I saw that one could be a horrible person, but if they turned in the numbers and made all the meetings, they were "in." But that thinking came and went, as I experienced it. When I left, it was during a time that I was trying to get back, as I had faded for awhile and I wanted to get back in. I was tying to make the meetings but kept missing them for various reasons. I had asked the Elders to set me up with a study with a spiritually strong sister. While waiting for this to happen, I had read over the Tuesday night book study article. It was the one about what blood fractions were acceptable and which ones were unacceptable. They even showed a graph that showed which was which. It made no sense to me. I kept meaning to get back to the Elders to ask about it, but kept missing meetings.

Finally, in a moment of frustration over it, I actually thought that surely some other JWs were confused about it. Surely some jw would have made a post on the Internet that would explain it so that I could understand it. So, I 'Googled' Jehovah's Witnesses and blood. I learned about the underground Elders, I think they are called AWARB, or something like - Elders who secretly are against the blood doctrine. I went to Wikipedia, and from there I learned about the U.N. connection, about passports, about Beth Sarim, I spent about three hours on the Internet getting my mind blown. Then, finally sat there with my head in my hands and said to myself, "Oh my God. I've just spent the last thirty years of my life in a cult. And I raised my kids in it, too."

So, it took one three hour session on the Internet to make me see the truth about "the truth." And from there, I just kept researching, quickly joined a forum, told my kids of my discoveries and husband, and to my surprise was met with negativity about what I had discovered. Then, my one daughter wanted to prove that what I had discovered was wrong, so she took some printouts I had brought to her and began to research for herself. She was a born in, so it took her about three months to finally be able to accept the facts.

What did you do different? Is your life better? Now, differently, my daughter and I enjoy celebrating holidays with her kids. I live with the freedom to be an independent thinker. I vote. I feel more connected to people in general, no longer looking at outsiders as being "worldly" as if that is a bad thing. I feel free to become friends with whomever I want to, to re-establish connections with old high school friends, without that nagging feeling that I shouldn't. There have been difficult times, shunning involved from the two daughters still in, but that has been resolved. There have been ups and downs, but now things are better than ever.

Van

What made you leave? Research was really the last straw for myself. When I left my mother's home and lived on my own, I stopped going to meetings, or really doing anything JWs do, but I still believed they were correct. When I started researching the goings on of the society, I discovered the numerous scandals that we all know so well. At that point, being young and naive, I assumed by simply informing my mother of these discoveries, she would realize the same thing I did. The way in which she defended her religion, even in the face of facts to the contrary, made me realize just how much of a harmful cult it is.

What did you do different? Pretty much everything. Starting with celebrating the holidays, making great friends among "the world", voting and watching TV/movies based on my interests, and not what could be "demonized". I eventually stopped believing in all religious claims and am still patiently waiting for any evidence of anything supernatural.

Is your life better? 100%. I no longer fear death or the consequences of a God punishing me for reading "the God Delusion". I married a like-minded woman and my life has honestly never been better. Discarding superstitious nonsense was the first step to truly living my life and it's been rewarding ever since.

Eewx2
What made you leave? I left for many reasons. I was sick of the rules. I wanted to celebrate holidays with my kids and family. I was sick of the lack of love. I was very "weak" spiritually, and the only help I got was to be told that I was going to die at Armageddon. The last event I attended was a Circuit Assembly and all the people who were supposed to be my brothers and sisters, were so very rude. After an agonizing six weeks of discussions with each other, my husband and decided to disassociate. After I left, I learned so many things that pointed to it being a cult. I have decided I am NEVER going back. So, I left for one reason and stay out for another.

What did you do different? Right away, I started celebrating birthdays and holidays. I started smoking and swearing (yeah, I know). My, um, bedroom life improved dramatically (hope I am allowed to say that). I threw out all my books and crap. I took all my dowdy meeting clothes out of my closet and eventually got rid of them. I fly the flag at national holidays. I finally got proper treatment for my Bipolar disorder. I reconnected with non J-dub family. I know there's a lot more but that's just off the top of my head.

Is your life better? By leaps and bounds! My husband and I no longer fight like we used to. By properly treating my mental illness I am a much calmer person. I no longer feel the pressure to be perfect for some organization. I do miss my parents, but through counseling, I am slowly but surely getting over it, although my counselor says I may never be totally over it.

Ceecee
What made you leave? I was a 3rd generation JW (the last!), and knew several genuinely lovely JWs. All that said, even as a kid I DESPISED the culture the Organization generated. Typically Witnesses I lived among were critical; small minded and generally self righteous. Sisters fawned over those with titles (or money), while avoiding the ones who most needed help. Brothers were frequently locked in a competition for positions of respect, rather than earning respect for their kindness toward others.

What did you do different? Just about everything.

At first, I tried living the "evil" life all worldly people were said to do. It wasn't as fun as it looked, and most of the so called worldly people I met were trying to live decent and honorable lives - better than many JWs I knew. I began taking night classes at the local branch of the State University. I LOVED using my mind, discussing new ideas and the next year, I quit my dead end job, sold all my stuff and headed to the main campus to finish my degree. It was a thrill! And guess what? I graduated; married a naval officer, had a career, and retired. Fifty-plus years after last hearing that Armageddon was coming soon it still hasn't come. Imagine all that I would have lost?

Is your life better? I've made a lot of mistakes by never having seen people deal with the problems of daily living outside the tyranny of a religion that does all the thinking for you. But overall I've lived a good, satisfying life. Something I'd never have been allowed under its demands. If my end comes tomorrow, I will be sorry to leave this life, but I can go in peace.

Gurgi

What made you leave? Well, i was really struggling at the time with extreme fatigue (M.E.) juggling work, meetings, auxiliary pioneering, mini serve stuff etc. Something had to give and that was my health. With my body and mind no longer able to cope, I had to keep working (couldn't get benefits). So, naturally meeting attendance and field service dropped. The way I was treated because of this was plain wrong.

I kept thinking of the woman who gave all she had (I forget the scripture - YAY!), and that surely Jehovah would understand. No, apparently not. I was hounded and eventually, after a meeting in my parents home (i still lived there), the presiding overseer raised his voice and had a go at me (my dad heard it all). I had a go back and it went from there really.

It was a distressing time, trying to wrap my (brainwashed), head around the uncaring nature of Jehovah's congregation. They lied about my being removed as a Ministerial servant, from the platform. I knew something was wrong and that this loving God I'd been taught about, just wouldn't do things like this.

I already had questions about hour counting (that had no scriptural basis whatsoever), and the way I was treated reaffirmed to me, that the organization was not about following the scriptures and their teachings but about counting hours. It didn't have any love and neither it seemed, did Jehovah, whom I prayed to every day.

What did you do different? Eventually, I was able to do simple but very important things, like get through one day, without feeling like God was going to kill me - turn off all of my lights at night, without feeling the devil or his demons were going to harm me, be able to collect records etc, without throwing them away for fear -

Basically, I lived with more freedom.

Is your life better? Yes. I understand a lot of things that i just didn't at the time. I'm able to cope with the realities each day brings. I've raised my daughter with a level of freedom I never imagined, and she tells me she loves me every day, because that's just how we are.

I have beers chilling in my fridge. Music to listen to tonight and a relaxed feeling in me, that was never there before. Long may it continue!

Section 2

Tales and other things.

Tales of the Borganisation.

Part 1
By Brother Grenzelos

An apostate, who was full of demons, stood on the Brooklyn Bridge. This loathsome creature was looking into the waters. A strange and fearful site met its evil eyes. A luminous patch floated mysteriously in the water.

The apostate screamed in agony as its body burned and turned to smouldering ash on the sidewalk.

Word reached the over fed, gluttonous, Governing Baddies. They all rose from their coffins and growled in hatred of the human race. Then, they levitated to their meeting room. After praising Satan and rubbing Masonic symbols on their nipples, they declared a state of 'Borgergency'.

Brother R Slicker banged his cross and crown decorated gavel, on the levitating, Pentangle table.

He began with ominous words, "J-Hoover's town, we have a problem!"

Brother Kiddy-Fiddler glared around the room, his head spinning round and round.

"Are there any recording devices in the room?" he boomed.

After a long pause, Brother Knorrs-Cheesesauce, confirmed he had used his X-ray vision. There were no recording devices in the room.

Brother Kiddy-Fiddler said, "Brothers, we have a leak!"

Brother Jackass exclaimed, "I'm sorry, it's my age!"

A deadly hush hung over the Satan approved meeting. Without a word, Brother Jackass realised he had committed a deadly error. Yes! A member of the Governing Baddies had apologised.

Never, in all their years of false predictions, 'new light' and 1975, had any paedophile protector on the GB, DARED to apologise.

Brother Jackass nervously acknowledged what he had done.

"I have apologised, a sin against the oily spirit, where do I stand?" he asked.

Brother Kiddy-Fiddler told him to take two paces forward. Then, to the left a bit and stand there. Whereupon, he pulled a big penis shaped leaver. Brother Jackass fell through a trapdoor and into Hades (the grave for Common people among mankind). Luckily, he was never seen again. Mind you, you could still smell him.

However, the WashTowel published an ingratiating article about the death of a faithful Brother, now in Hellven etc etc.

The meeting continued. Brother Kiddy-Fiddler resumed his explanation.

"Some oily spirit has come from Jar-Hoover. Sad to say, it has leaked into the river! Someone has been to the toilet too soon after eating some oily spirit. The crap from the 'excreting saliva cl-arse' member has spillethed into the river, instead of being printed in the Dublications. Brothers. I say we need to establish how such a leak happened. On the flip side, the good news is, it destroyed a mentally diseased apostate, who was worldly and not in the truth," said Kiddy-Fiddler, as he handed out child pornography to the others.

Brother Clenchbuttock had a brilliant explanation.

"We'll tell all the Brothers in the Borganization, that we are 'just imperfect men and make mistakes'. Yes, we have oily spirit but sometimes lose it," said Clenchbuttock, accepting the child pornography with glee.

Brother Kiddy-Fiddler smiled the kind of smile a shark gives, when you dip your toes in the water.

Thus, it was unanimous. From thence, it was decreed that any errors, deaths of innocent sheeple, because of errors and 'old light', would be explained away in this manner. Thus, there would never again be the need for an apology from the Bored of Defectors AKA the Grovelling Buddy, AKA the Governing Baddies AKA Paedophile Ring.

A special letter was sent to 'all bodies of Eldubs', explaining that it was every one Else's fault! No blame for the cult leaders, when anything bad happened. The holy leaders are directed by oily spirit but it sometimes gets flushed down the toilet!

This was to be read during the 'Local needs' item, as scheduled monthly, in the King Dumb Mockery. (It carried the instruction – May we encourage all in attendance to swallow any lies we tell and remain in a zombiefied hypnotic state - yadda, yadda, yadda).

Meanwhile, some demons do some stuff.

to be CULTinued

Experiences you won't find in the Yearbook.

Following on from the interviews with funny moments, I thought it would be nice to share some more 'experiences'.

At every JW convention we waited with bated breath for encouraging 'real life stories' to show how JWs were just the coolest. Here however, I wish to share some true accounts that are for your delectation and amusement.

These didn't make the Conventions or Yearbooks.

***

The Brother was giving a talk about how we demonstrate politeness and respect for Jehovah and others, by switching our phones off at the meetings.

A few minutes into the talk his rang.

***

While discussing a Kingdom Hall refurbishment, three brothers on the platform, were asking about the colour scheme, when one of the older ones there piped up that we'd need a dildo rail around the wall.

***

A nervous Brother went on the ministry with Brother Bull. On a return visit, his introduction was, "I've brought my bull with me today."

***

We were all encouraged by the brave Sister who missed the meeting. She had been picking apples but had slipped from the ladder. The brave Sister revealed the horrific story in her comment, at the next meeting.

"The devil did it. He pushed me off the ladder, so I missed the meeting."

***

Picture the beautiful British countryside of rural Cambridgeshire. A local pub has a sculpted hedge outside. It is in the shape of a man. Vandals had cut its arm off one night.

Local Brother Angry speaks to a householder, near the armless hedge. He points to the armless man and asks the householder, "You know who did that?"
"No."
"Londoners. That's who!"
"I'm a Londoner," replied the householder.

No placements were made. How happifying.

***

A Jamaican householder told the Brother, "I know the name of god. It's Jehoviah."

The Brother also of Jamaican roots, then lectured the householder about the pronunciation of the name 'Jehovah'. This lecture went on for some time. He told the householder that there was no 'i' in the divine name.

There were no placements made and no return visit was arranged. How happifying.

***

The French Brother had the grand privilege of commenting during the Watchtower study.

We were very happified to hear how the apostles had to travel through 'hot dessert country.'

Perhaps he meant 'hot desert country'. But the thought of the apostles eating warm chocolate puddings seemed more realistic.

***

A Vietnamese brother in a spoke very broken English. He didn't really know American slang and didn't realize that some words were curse words. He gave a comment at the book study. It wasn't clear what he was trying to say but he said 'bullsh1t'. Much hilarity ensued.

***

The old Sister with the wig fell asleep during the meeting. Her head fell back. Her wig landed on the lap of Sister Snooty. Sister Snooty jumped up and exclaimed, "There's a pussy on my lap!"

The attendant calmly replaced the wig crookedly, back on the head from whence it originated.

***

The old Brother told us how he was encouraged by older Watchtower articles.

He said, "I love looking up back passages."

***

The Brother strode onto the platform majestically. He began with a rousing introduction.
"I'm a man and so is my wife," he said.

He paused and continued, "who doesn't like to see cruelty to animals."

He looked at the audience.

"Why are you laughing, Brothers?" he asked.

***

Brother Insane was on the ministry. He presented a magazine that mentioned the witnessing work in Japan.

The householder was horrified with his introduction.

"There are many JWs in Japan. Do you know why?" he asked.

The householder was silent.

"Because we dropped the bomb on them. That's why," the Brother said thumping his fist into the palm of his hand for emphasis.

No magazines were placed. How happifying.

***

Poor Brother Timid wasn't at home on the platform but did his best.

He handled an item that told us we should be 'mature Christians.' In a trembling voice, he said, "We must be manure."

***

In the UK, a young Brother told us how good Jehovah's organisation is.

"We are thankful for Jehovah's orgasm," he said.

***

Brother Payne was sitting in the back portion of the Kingdom Hall. The Elder conducting the meeting called on him to answer by saying, "Brother Payne in the rear."

***

There is the encouraging account of the Brother that commented in the Watchtower study, about Homosexuality. He used to be in the Royal Navy and referred back to those days.

What he meant to say was: "If a gay man propositioned me, I would punch them in the face."

What he actually said was, "If a homosexual approached me, I'd give him a good fisting!"

I was the only one in the meeting laughing. But then, meetings were no laughing matter.

***

How efficacious to reflect upon the Ministry school talk in which the brother got to cover the topic of "pronunciation". He enunciated the word very carefully, over and over again - 'repetition for emphasis' and all that!

The problem was, he pronounced 'pronunciation' wrong every time.

"PRO NOWN SEE AY SHUN!"

***

The German Sister was preparing for the Convention at the Football stadium.

She told the Elder that she likes to sit in the seats at the top of the stadium.

"Why is that?" asked the Elder.
"Because I get ze wind," she replied in a German accent.
"Perhaps you should take some 'Rennies' to ease it," replied the Elder, thinking she had gas.
"Nein! I get ze wind. It blows over ze field und into ze stand!"

***

The talk that included: "Jehovah allows us to learn by our mistakes sometimes. Like on the way over here to give this talk, I got a speeding ticket."

***

Delegates at a Convention in the USA were delighted to hear that an octopus has 8 testicles.

***

In the sign language congregation, a hearing brother was talking about the problems in the world, the cost of living, the price of fuel. He used the sign for petrol, and didn't understand why so many deaf sign language users were sniggering away. Afterwards he was kindly told that he has used the sign for "f*cking is so expensive these days."

***

An experience not in the Spanish yearbook.

During a convention a Brother from an English speaking Bethel came to give a talk in Spanish - not his first language. He made a remark, which is a really nice way of calling someone an asshole in Spanish. He said, "Jehova no tiene madre." And everyone in the convention hall either started to laugh or was utterly shocked.

***

An Elder was reading the Watchtower. It said, "we must fight the hard fight of the faith."

Instead of saying 'hard fight,' he said, "hard FART."

***

In ASL (sign language) they modify the sign Bible for their own unique sign. Original sign in formal ASL is "Jesus book". Our contributor notes: "I always would sign the original way so people would understand what was going on."

Tales of the Borganisation.
Part 2

Situation Vacant

Wanted : Servant

Due to the apostasy of one of our members, a servant is required. The successful applicant will have a proven track record of licking Elder's boots.

Perks include: Microphone handling. Reading the Watchtower. Looking down with scorn on publishers if they have not highlighted their watchtowers. Collection of money for the Governing Body by guilt, fear and phobia.
Wives must be in submission and submit to the bigheadship of the applicant.

Apply: Jehovah or write direct to the Co-ordinator of the Body of Holy Holy GB worshippers Glazedlook Congregation of Jehovah's witnesses. Tel: 01233 05666 13311

Three demons sat in the sky looking over the edge of a cloud. They wondered if they should magically become human and shag some repressed Sisters in fine standing. Although they had never though of this before, they had read about it in a WashTowel Dublication and thought it sounded fun. They laughed as the miserable faced Brothers in fine standing, and Sisters in fine standing, sloped into the dull, rectangular, austere and damp Spindom Hall. It is a cold Sunday morning in January. The world is dead. Everybody in the hall wish they were dead too.

It is many years since Armageddon™ didn't arrive in October 1975 as promised. But that's Okay. Jar-Hoover is obviously a liar because of imperfect men.

Strange crop circles had appeared in the field next door. This was clearly the work of worldly apostates who were not in the truth, but full of demons instead.

The local chemist was out walking his dog. They passed the Spindom Hall.

He said a cheery 'Hello!' to all those going in. He knew them all quite well because they were ALL his best customers. They regularly came in to pick up their Prozac prescriptions.

Without them he'd be out of business. How he loved 'Jar-Hoover's HAPPY pill PEOPLE!'

A strange, shadowy, heap of crap approached the prattform, in the hall. No, wait. Is it a turd? Is it a pain? No. It's super - I mean Brother Stubcock!

Stubcock called the meeting to order. He was a sweaty, obese man, with 1980's style spectacles made of brown plastic and mended in the middle with a band aid. He could hardly see through his specs as he was too lazy to clean them. When he did it, was just to wipe them with his gelatinous mucus and bogey encrusted hanky. His hair was so greasy that he looked like he had washed it in a deep fat fryer and combed it with a beef burger. Perhaps that's how he got the chip on his shoulder.

His favourite food being slices of water melon. He thought himself so clever for calling those slices 'spindom frowns'. This was because they were curved and when turned up side down resembled the depressed mouth of Brothers in fine standing.

If he had a penny for each time he'd told that joke, he'd be rich. If he lost a penny for each time a Brother thought he was simply being a pious twit, he'd owe a lot of money, (similar in proportions to the amount the Borganisation was paying out for child abuse lawsuits).

He glared around the Spindom Hall at the yellowing wallpaper, mildew curtains and crappy carpet. He gave a fake smile and spoke.

"Although it's cold outside, we give you a warm (polite but not genuine laughter), welcome, Brothers in fine standing, Sisters in fine standing and fronds, to the Glazedlook CON-gregation Spindom Hall of Jar-Hoover's witnesses. If you could be finding your seats, although how you could have lost them in the first place baffles me, given the size of a chair.
Before we invoke our visiting sneaker, Brother Bummer, to the prattform, it is appropriate as always, to sing a song of prose to Jar-Hoover.

The song chosen by our favourite Bummer, is based on those beautiful words, found in the prophetic book in the Oily Bile; 1 Paedophile 3:4. Song number 69 entitled, 'Ever loyal to men not Jar-Hoover'. So, stand whether you are able or not, and sing along. Er, song 69."

Before Stubcock had finished talking, the dreadful tinkle of the out of tune piano starts. The music resembled the sound of a dentist's drill and a screaming patient, as if heard from behind the dentist's door. How he glowers at the Brother on the sound desk. The whole congo-abongo observed Stubcock (the Cock-up-ordinator of the baddy of Eldubs), show his disdain for Minnyserves in this way.

In the captive audience (peak attendance 7), a wicked sod who has apostate leanings and uses the evil Internet, thought such a rudeness was wrong. All the other Brothers in fine standing and Sisters in fine standing admired Stubcock. Oh, how holy he is. So commanding. He must be better than Jar-Hoover itself.

The song tinkled on and the Brothers in fine standing and Sisters in fine standing groan along to the soulless crap. Those that were not comatose by now, soon would be when Stubcock droned the opening prayer to magic sky daddy. Luckily, this prayer wasn't as long as normal because he couldn't sum up the whole bloody spiritless meeting in it.

It went along the lines of:"Oooooooh, Jar-HooooOOOOOOooooover. May we reproach you in flairs, before your throne of unreserved blindness. May your oily spirit rest on all those taking part...yadda, yadda, yadda.... thank the filthful saliva cl-arse....yadda, yadda, yadda.......look forward to the WashTowel study.... yadda, yadda, yadda...this time of the end.. yadda, yadda, yadda...do more in the ministry or die.. yadda, yadda, yadda.....look forward to a very boring talk.... yadda, yadda, yadda....pay close attention... yadda, yadda, yadda....healthful turds... yadda, yadda, yadda......only the Borganization has the tooth... yadda, yadda, yadda.....let us give the cult leaders lots of money…blah, blah, blah…..in Cheeses lame, Airmen!"

Stubcock introduced the pubic balk entitled: 'Happy though hungry, after giving all your money to the Borganisation!'

Bummer gets on the prattform. A wannabe mini man adjusts the microphone, which is still turned on and feeds back. An unpleasant sound, but not as bad as the dog awful 'Humdrum Melodies'.

Meanwhile, in the Brooklyn bunker Brother Gnaw makes a startling discovery that adds new odour to the urine patches on the crotch of his blue nylon trousers.

to be CULTinued (Perhaps. Armageddon™ permitting)

Thanks to **Mandy** for this cartoon.

Tales of the Borganisation.
Part 3

Untold miles under Brooklyn HQ, a desiccated old twit of a Brother, and sits in his lead lined bunker. Lugubriously, he is perusing pornography, over his half moon spectacles. He is wearing a blue nylon suit and has a grubby brown knitted tie.

He looks up at the clock as the second hand counts slowly towards Armageddon™ (which will be soon now).

"It's time for a break," he muses, as he scratches the scabs off his rectum, which is situated under his nose. Perhaps that's why he needed breath mints.

He reaches for another glass of virgin's blood. He takes a sip. Then he decides to read something under the 'humour' section, in his theo-twotic library. He reaches feebly, for an older copy of the WashTowel and Harold of Chrysler's Pheasants.

He closes his eyes and asks Beelzebub for help to find a crap ridden article.

By the soft light of a passing demon, he falls upon an uninteresting piece of writing.

For what seems seconds, he reads the rubbish that some twit who knew naff all about the Bile (Yes. I said BILE not Bible. This is supposed to be an ironic parody), had written. His mouth drops open in utter surprise, as the realization of something hits him like an apostate custard pie in the face of someone in the 'Truth™'.

Scurrying like the rat, he is he grabs the 'twot phone'. His deathline to the Governing Baddies of Filthful Saliva members. The answer at the other end comforts him and makes his nuts feel nice and tingly. He thinks of child pornography and how the Borganisation has protected him from the police. He smiles.

The voice says, 'Please hold. Your call is of no importance to us. All calls are recorded for straining and disfellowshipping purposes. We know you are waiting and someone will be with you as soon as they rise from the grave!'

Suddenly, he hears, 'Is that you Brother Gnaw?'

He replies, "Tis I, Oh, evil one. Brother Gnaw at your cervix!"
"I told you never to call me here, unless it's a diarrheic borgergency!"
"But Brother Kiddy-Fiddler, it IS a borgergency. I have bumbled across something that could damage the already terrible reputation of Jar-Hoover's Borganization!"
"Never may that happen! As Satan is our real leader, this cannot be so. Speak man, what is it!"

Trembling all over (but not the knees as knee tremblers are not allowed), Brother Gnaw speaks.
"Please don't send me to Hades (the common gravy of ham rind), but I have discovered and old WashTowel article that has, that has -"
"Speak up man I haven't got all overlapping generations to wait!"
"Erm. The WashTowel printed a TRUTH!"

There is silence at the other end of the twot phone.

A roar of Satanic laughter (normally forbidden), ring from Brother Kiddy-Fiddler.

"That is not a problem. Just calm down, Gnaw. Remember we are imperfect men, directed by Jar-Hoover's oily spirit. We can simply blame it on the 'Udder Sheeple'. Yes. They will take full blame, just like they did when we lied about 1975. That is all. Satan prevails!"

With a great weight lifted from his shoulders (he never knew why he carried an anvil on his back), Brother Gnaw drifts back into his brainless hypnotic state, once again content he will live forever in Hellven not a Paradox Girth, where all the second class udder sheeple will be herded.

He looked forward to another night in his bunker, protected by Lucifer and laid in a coffin, lined with earth from his hometown. Cockfosters in London.

And they probably do!

to be CULTinued (Perhaps. Armageddon™ permitting…who knows?)

You could be an ex JW……..

if the only song you know by Jimi Hendrix is - (fill in the blank)

if you are under the illusion Hank Marvin can actually play the guitar.

if you think the Shadows and Prince would make a great super group.

if the time 'half past eight' frightens you because it sounds like Apostate!

if you look around for a spy before wishing a happy birthday.

if you have never seen 'the Exorcist' or 'Harry Potter' movies.

if every time you see 6.07 on a digital clock you think of 5.39.

if you find yourself thinking, 'I must look that up.'

if you clean windows or cars for a living and still own five suits.

if you think 2-door vehicles aren't really cars.

if you can't buy a pair of shoes without thinking about how comfortable they will need to be while walking residential streets.

if you refer to books by colour instead of by title.

if you can't pick up a book, without picking up a ruler or highlighter too.

if you no longer suffer from 'cognitive dissonance'.

if after a "get-together" at your home, your house is not a mess and you have more food than when you started.

If you think things are getting worse in the world, and you're thrilled.

if you voted for the first time after nearly fifty years and felt guilty.

if your small children know that Father Christmas isn't real.

if you squirm at love scenes, swearing or blasphemy in movies or ALL of Life of Brian.

if someone says "knock knock", instead of replying, "who's there?" you offer them magazines.

if you're not afraid of dying, just how "the god of love" will destroy you.

if Black pudding is a worry.

if you have a hard time grasping that "no trespassing" really does refer to you.

if you watch movies and TV shows that show New York and you look for the Watchtower buildings.

if you instinctively open a Bible to Psalms 83:18.

if you think you should be somewhere on a Sunday morning, but can't think where.

if the word "apostate" terrifies you.

if you can hold 2 contradictory beliefs and still think both are true.

Tales of the bOrganisation reloaded

It had been raining in the night. Brother Skeptick had hoped it'd be peeing it down Saturday morning. Unfortunately, the sun came up, the birds tweeted in the trees and he had to go on the ministry. No excuses this time. No rain to remove the guilt he felt for not forcing the ClockTower onto 'worldly' people (that Jar-Hoover would murder at Armageddon).

He checked the 'Day's text', in case the overbearing study overseer asked his usual pompous 'I know more than you' questions, about the inane drivel contained in the text.

No doubt, it would be the usual Saturday's 'do more in the ministry or be murdered by God. There would be the usual 'feel guilty', couched in a rosy sounding sc-rupture, that had a totally different meaning.

A breakfast of Cornflukes and nausea was swilled down with coffee. As a member of Jar-Hoover's Happy-pill People, our Brother took some Valium.

The meeting was cold, spiritless and yet another attempt to encourage recruiting into the publishing business.

The gluttonous, overbearing oversneer did indeed, ask questions only designed to make himself look superior. He handed out the terror-try and arranged for those who loathed each other to work together.

He really was a twot and there are plenty like him!

Our Brother dragged his feet along Bumstead Road (even numbers with 34, 36, 38 as a DNC). His partner, a young Brother, Ezra Keen, was full of spunk in so many ways.

"This week's ClockTower is so encouraging. The best yet," said Keen.

"Yes! They're always better than the last one," replied Skeptick.

Keen was unsure what Skeptick meant. But unabashed continued spouting cult nonsense.
"Yes, the 'New Light' is truly exciting about 'over flapping germinations'. Sowing the seed! It couldn't get any better," he waffled.
"The lies get brighter!"
"Oh, sounded like you said 'lies' there for a minute! Ha, ha!"
"Oh, ha, ha! I'm the ClockTower reader this week..what joy."
"Oh, wow. What a grand privilege of unity in this time of the end as we go our separate ways, so that's fine isn't it!'
"What a shame. It's starting to rain. Oh, well, see you tomorrow! I'm off home!"
"OK. Nice working with you, but it's not raining."
"Yeah, but you lot are a real shower. I can't stand this anymore, no offence but you can read the ClockTower for me instead. I'm off, give the Brothers my love and tell them to do more research on the Internet about ClockTower history. You too!"

Thus a happy ending for both Brothers.

Keen went on to be a regular reader of the ClockTower and would bend over backwards for the overseers (especially behind closed doors).

Skeptick went of to join the Atheist Army. He was last seen marching toward Brooklyn on 05/11/2017 with his troop of 'Apostates'.

True story. Well, if you believe stuff you read in the WashTowel, then this qualifies as factual.

Tales of the…..well, you know by now….

The coaches began to arrive at the 'Bunghole Glory Football Stadium' after 8:31am. They were forbidden to arrive at 8:30am as this was 'half past eight', which sounded like 'apostate'.

Wearing their best 'meeting clothes', adorned with pentacle delegate name badges, the Jar-Hoover's dooflops alighted the coaches and filed into the stadium. They dragged their poor children behind them. The kids were expected to sit for hours, listening to the boring talks, without so much as a silent fart.

Unbeknown to them, high on the hill, stood a haunted mansion. It was called, 'Beth Serum'. It was six miles to the west. A storm was brewing. Lightening cracked and flashed around the towers of the mansion. A shadowy, cloaked figure peered from the lead lighted window, in the highest tower. His name was Spektacula, king of the mentally diseased apostates.

He had once belonged to Jar-Hoovers Grovelling body but had been bitten on the neck by the Internet, which caused his death. However, in the 'twinkling of an eye', his eyes had twinkled. Then, he was resurrected, as a disfellowshipped person. He was the first of a new breed of strange creatures that inhabited the forbidden zone, known in hushed Jar-Hoover circles, as 'the world'.

Yes! Spektacula was an apostate. He was not in the truth and was very 'worldly'. Bloody hell, it felt good!!

Back at the stadium, the victims, er, faithful, began to sit on the splintering, damp, haemorrhoid inducing, wooden benches. During these excruciating two days, they would receive piles of awful new releases to unleash on the public, and piles up the bum too.

The arse-embly chairman welcomed everyone to the 'Obey us or die!' convention. He promised how 'stimulating and up building' it would be. Most would be stimulated to sleep or dream of sex with someone who wasn't their spouse. This was because the ClockTower's bedroom rules forbade sex between married couples full stop! Everyone was so repressed they might just explode!

All in attendance were ordered to stand and sing with enthusiasm, a bloody awful 'humdrum melody'. Why they were called 'melodies' no one knew. There was no discernible melody, just the sound of an orchestra in the strains of, either dying, or tuning up. The song was all about obedience to the Grovelling body, rather than God. Admittedly, God gets a passing mention in the songs, but nothing to make him appear superior to the perverted Grovelling Baddies.

As always, the song was supposedly based on a scripture, to add a mystical quality to it. In reality, it was some verse taken out of context and nothing to do with the actual song. Who would know? No one ever checked, and if they did, they faced disfellowshipping for asking questions.

The Brother said a long prayer, to start the meeting. He used all his best theo-twotic jargon. Things such as: 'in the tooth', 'filthful saliva', 'kill all apostates', 'obey Jar-Hoover or die', 'appreciate the grand privilege in this time of the end' and other painful expressions invented to subjugate the 'flock' or bore them to mindlessness.

Six miles away, Spektakula had summoned his minions.

He addressed them:
"The time is here. At last it is time to attack the Witlesses and persecute them! Yes, Armageddon will begin. We will march on their convention. Let the 'Great Troubleation' begin!"

With that, the creatures were magically flown by 'Sexually Experienced Airways', to the convention. They all parachuted into the stadium. Thus adding interest to the costumed drama. This was the only place where beards were allowed on the prattform. Even the Brothers could wear one too. How happifying. Some apostates missed the stadium and landed in the river, which was okay. It simply dampened their enthusiasm.

The apostates were in!

Part 2

The costumed traumatisation (about some obscure and irrelevant Bile character who did something or other, that makes us all want to recruit others into the cult), was enacted.

A heap of grease, wearing glasses, stood proudly in front of the microphone. He addressed the assembled masses. His comb-over blowing across his glasses in the breeze. The title of his talk was: 'New light, how much more can we take before the bulb blows?'

Yes! Brother Stubcock was on the prattform at the arse-embly. Such honour. Such prestige. Such self serving balderdash.

He observed with pious sneering arrogance (not to be confused with 'pioneering arrogance'. That is reserved for Eldubs who knock on doors a lot, forgetting Luke 10:7), as the apostates entered the stadium.

He bellowed over the sound system:
"'Witness to the apostates! Convert them to the Borganization at all costs! At the same time, shun them!
Get experiences as we are running low on them and have had to invent them. Place gammy-zines with them! Get free home ClockTower non Oily Bile studies. Show fake love and sham concern for them! Forward you witlesses ever strong of heart - !!!!"

He began to pray so earnestly, that Jar-Hoover couldn't wait to kill him at Armageddon.

"OoooOOOooooOOOOooooh, Jar-Hooooooooooooooooooooover GAAAAAWD. Please, Oh, Lard let us have a good day in the ministry this day. OOOooooOOOOooooOOOOoooooh, we beseech thee oh Lard, to take away the stumbling block of apostasy…"

Suddenly, a foaming keg of beer fell from the sky. It killed Brother Stubcock. Jar-Hoover had had enough. The corpse of Stubcock was covered in bubbling beer. The froth of the gods!

Seeing opportunities to get some hours, to put on the monthly report slips, the witlesses commenced theo-twatic warfare. Book bags and litter-trash trolleys were flung in all directions.

Satan frowned as a passing UFO, from the inter-dimensional planet Apostus, flew over. It was disguised as a 'fake plane hologram' and forgot to leave a 'mind controlling chem trail' over the stadium. Which was just as well. Why waste mind altering chemicals when the Washtowel Babylon Crap Society did it with words.

An old Brother, Dick Less, who had seen 1914, full of zeal and self righteousness, approached an apostate creature. The Brother began his attack. Holding his ClockTower and Asleep! gammy-zines, in the shape of a stake.

"My friend and I, are making a brief and friendly call on you and your neighbours," he began, as the apostate froze in its tracks.

He continued, "I am asking, have you ever wondered why things are so bad in the world? Oh, they are so bad, so deadly, deadly bad, beyond redemption bad. Oh, so bloody terribly bad beyond reason, bad. We all wonder why the world didn't explode in 1975 bad. Many are concerned that in this very neighbourhood, a man was heard to have been stopped for speeding in his car. 1 MPH over the speed limit. Did you know God will kill him and all his young children at Armageddon if he doesn't accept a ClockTower gammy-zine?"

The apostate was confused and responded, "I want to know, how can I be saved from God murdering me? Where else will I go?"

"Jar-Hoover has nothing to do with this. You have to join our destructive mind controlling cult and serve the Grovelling body, in blind obedience. You will need to get craptized into the Borganization and work your buttocks off, recruiting and getting money for the 'Protect a pervert fund'. You will have guilt, fear and phobia induced on you if you even think a non ClockTower approved thought."

"Well, as I hate God anyway, it's a fair cop!"

It was a miracle! The apostate's skin turned from green to a Jar-Hoover approved colour scheme. His eyes glazed over as he began to give a supercilious smile. His name changed to Andre. A JW.Org logo appeared on his lapel.

An 'experience' was beheld, first hand, by all at the arse-embly. It didn't need exaggerating, when it was 're-enacted' at a boring Circus arse-embly! An apostate was converted back to the Borganization. However, he wasn't told he'd have to sit at the back of the Spindom Hall, be treated like dirt, with no one talking to him for at least a year.

Meanwhile in row 6 (an earthly number), an apostate cornered an anointed Sister.

"Fancy a drink?" asked the creature.
"Go on then," she replied.

The creature handed her a recipe card. On it was written the following:

RECIPE FOR AN APOSTATE COCKTAIL

The Blood Transfusion.

Half fill a highball glass with tomato juice.

Add 25ml Southern Comfort and 25ml White rum.

Bung in a dollop of Tabasco sauce or West Indian hot pepper sauce. If you're a wuss, soy sauce.

Place a segment of water melon (Kingdom smile), on the glass.

………or just buy a crate of beers.

"I'll have the cocktail," she said.
"Why?"
"It's full of spirit."

There was no applause. Some tumbleweed rolled by.

Real Kingdom Maladies

Singing and Accompanying Yourselves with More Soup and Your Artichoke Hearts

These are the Kingdom songs™ (Old and new), renovated with food titles.

1. Jehovah's artichokes

2. We thank you Jello shots

3. God is Clove

4. Making a Good Naan with God.

5. Crisps, Our Exemplar

6. The Praline of God's Servant

7. Christian Daddojanam

8. The Lord's Evening Meal™

9. Praise Genoa , Our god

10. Here I am, Send Meat

11. Making Genoa's Heart Glazed

12. The Choux Marmite Maiden

13. Keep Your Fries on the Pies

14. Balsamic Vinegar in Gilead

15. The Marinade of the Lamb

16. See Yourself When all is Stew

17. Bless our Meat Tin Together

18. Praise Jam Jar with me

19. Shepherd's pie - gifts in menu

20. Loyal Submission to cheese and cracker Orders

21. From hummus to hummus

22. This is the whey

23. Ever oil

24. God's wondrous woks

25. Cod is love

26. The noodle song

27. Loyal loaf

Genesis-ish.
The forgotten chapters.

Translated from the original Tea brew by Brother Grenzelos

1. In the beginning the Governing Body of Jehovah's witnesses created heaven and earth. Hell, they even decided on a name for the god they invented too. Their franchise was ready to go.

And the Watchtower proceeded to be formless and a waste. Nothing has changed. It's pretty much still a waste.

And the Governing Body said, "Let there be New Light™." There proceeded to be unbelievable claims from the Watchtower. The Governing Body saw that the stupid claims were good.

The Governing Body said, "Give us your money that we may fight lawsuits."

And the Governing Body said, "Let the congregations teem with idiots that will give us money and power."

2. And the cult was completed in its array.

And the Governing Body sat on their fat, gluttonous backsides and laughed at all they had accomplished.

And Lo! It was money making. And the governing body enjoyed all the worship and prestige their cult gave them.

3. Now, the Governing Body proved to be narcissistic and wicked. The 'apostates™' came along and exposed the evil of the Governing Body.

And Lo! The Governing Body were not happy bunnies.

And the Governing Body said, "Shun everyone that does not worship us and give us money."

And families were destroyed and lives wasted in the wake of the selfishness of the Governing Body.

And the media told stories of the pain the Governing Body had inflicted through their delusional lies.

4. And the Holy, Holy, Holy Governing Body haven't changed. They still demand worship, money and assets.

And the Lawsuits said, "We will bruise you in the wallet, and you will not get away with protecting perverts in your cult."

And Lo! The Governing Body were not happy bunnies.

……………………………………GOOD!

Relevation
The forgotten bits.

Translated from the original Creep by Brother Grenzelos

1. The relevation from the Governing Body, which Delusion gave them to show their servants what must soon take place.
  The Delusion made it known by sending money to his gods, the Holy, Holy, Holy Governing Body, who testifies to everything that gives them cash — that is, the world of Delusion and the testimony of the Holy, Holy, Holy Governing Body.

2. I warn everyone who hears the words of the prophecy of this weird cult: If anyone adds anything to the watchtower or publications, the Governing Body will add to that person the shunning described in the secret Elder's 'Flock book'.
  And if anyone takes words away from the Watchtower corporation, the Holy, Holy, Holy Governing Body will take away from that person any share in the treacle of life and in the cult compound of Warwick, which is pretty darned nice. Ideal for cult leaders to live their rock star lifestyle.
  He who testifies to these things says, "Yes, I am coming to get your cash again soon."
  Amen. Come, Governing Body.
  The hatred of the Watchtower corporation be with the cult's people. Amen.

Section 3

Glossary

Terms used by JWs and their meanings in simple terms

The Truth	What JW's call their religion/Watchtower corporation dogma. It is also a description of being a member of Watchtower corporation. IE. To be 'in the truth' = to be a JW
1914	The date the Watchtower corporation says Jesus returned to Earth but was invisible
1780 1798 1799 1829 1840 1844 1846 1872 1874 1878 1880 1881 1891 1906 1910 1914 1915 1917	Dates the end of the world was predicted and later denied, mostly

1918	
1920	
1921	
1925	
1926	
1928	
1932	
1935	
1940s	
1951	
1975	
144,000	Amount of humans going to heaven (Not symbolic)
Accurate Knowledge	Only Watchtower doctrine
Anointed	A JW that thinks god has chosen them to go to heaven rather than live on Paradise earth
Apostate	Pejorative term. A word changed by the JWs to mean a person that has left the Watchtower corporation. These ones are shunned (even by close family), and vilified
Assembly	Large gathering of congregations

Awake!	A magazine distributed by JWs
Babylon the great	Non Watchtower corporation religions/cults
Bad association	Someone that does not obey Watchtower corporation rules
Baptism	Full water immersion to show allegiance to Watchtower corporation
Bethel	Headquarters of the corporations
Bible study	Process of indoctrination using Watchtower corporation publications. Also refers to a non JW that is being indoctrinated by Watchtower corporation dogma
Bible-Trained Conscience	Obeying Watchtower corporation rules

Brotherhood	Only JWs
Brotherly Love	Conditional love based on obedience to Watchtower corporation rules
Brother/s	Male JW/s (Usually 'baptised')
Buying out the opportune time	Spending time working for Watchtower corporation interests
Christendom	All Christian religions that are not the Watchtower corporation
Circuit Assembly	Large gathering of congregations
Circuit Overseer	Watchtower corporation company man in charge of a 'circuit'
Congregation	Designated group of JWs that meet together
Contribution	Money given to the Watchtower corporation
Convention	Large gathering of congregations
Demonistic	Someone with a mental illness or something not approved by Watchtower corporation
Demonized	Someone with a mental illness or something not approved by Watchtower corporation
Demons	Invisible magical creatures that JWs fear
Disassociation or DA/ed	When someone does not wish to be a JW anymore they are to be shunned. This is a control method used to prevent ones from leaving or giving Watchtower corporation a bad name. Disassociated ones must be ignored and shunned. Watchtower corporation recommends this practice to break up families where they deem corporation policies are violated

Disfellowshipping or DF/ing	A control method used to prevent ones from leaving or giving Watchtower corporation a bad name. Disfellowshipped ones must be ignored and shunned. Watchtower corporation recommends this practice to break up families where they deem corporation policies are violated

We appreciate the grand privilege of unity, in this time of the end, as we go our separate ways.

District	An area covering several 'circuits'
District Assembly	Large gathering of congregations
District Convention	Large gathering of congregations

District Overseer	Watchtower corporation company man in charge of a district
Elders	Local leaders
Encourage/ment	Reminders to obey Watchtower corporation rules
Faith	Believing what Watchtower corporation says
Faithful and Discreet Slave	A title (from the Bible), that the corporation leaders give themselves
Faithful Christians	Only JWs
Faithful slave	A title (from the Bible), that the corporation leaders give themselves
Fear of man	Not obeying Watchtower corporation rules because of a non JW's opinion
Field ministry	Door knocking
Field service	Door knocking
Field Service Time	Counting how many hours one spends in the 'ministry'. This is to buy salvation and so the Elders can judge one's 'spirituality'
Generation	A fluctuating period of time. The length of a generation depends upon Watchtower corporation doctrine at the current time
Getting time in	Buying salvation by handing in a 'report slip'
Gilead	Watchtower corporation school
Goal	'Reporting' the amount of 'hours' set by self or Watchtower corporation
Goats/Goat like ones	All of mankind that are not JWs
God's Channel (of communication)	Watchtower corporation

Good news of the Kingdom	Watchtower corporation doctrine
Good news of the Kingdom	Watchtower corporation doctrine
Governing Body	A title (NOT from the Bible), that the godlike corporation leaders give themselves
Great Crowd	Non 'anointed' JWs that will live on 'paradise earth' after 'Armageddon'.
Great tribulation	A supposed time when all JWs will be persecuted for staying loyal to Watchtower corporation. This is said to be just before 'Armageddon'
Honest-Hearted-ones	Only Jehovah's witnesses
Honour	An honour = Being allowed to do some drudge for the Watchtower corporation. To be honoured = A state of praise

Hours	To qualify for eternal life in 'paradise', a JW must report how many hours they have spent in the 'ministry' each month
Householder	Non JW met on the door knocking work.
Inactive	A JW that is not reporting 'hours' to the Elders
Incidental witnessing	See: Informal witnessing
Informal witnessing	Talking to a non JW about Watchtower dogma in an effort to recruit them
In gathering work	Converting ones to allegiance to the

	Watchtower corporation
Integrity keeper	One that obeys Watchtower corporation
Irregular /publisher	One that does not hand in a 'report' regularly each month
Jehovah	Watchtower corporation's name for god
Jehovah's chariot	Watchtower corporation
Jehovah's Happy People	Only Jehovah's witnesses
Jehovah's Organization	Watchtower corporation and legal entities
Jehovah's Theocratic Arrangement	Watchtower corporation and legal entities
Judicial committee/hearing	Kangaroo court to reprimand those not obeying the laws of Watchtower corporation
JW	Jehovah's witness
Kingdom Hall	Meeting place of JWs
Kingdom Ministry	Door knocking also a title of an internal leaflet JWs have
Kingdom interests	Pertains to Watchtower corporations possessions and rules
Last days	Current period of time. Watchtower corporation say that 'Armageddon' is coming soon
Literature	Magazines, books, leaflets and tracts
Literature cart/trolley	A manned 'vending' device to advertise and distribute Watchtower corporation literature (Bibles are hidden from the cart/trolley)
Little flock	Those that believe they will go to heaven. Number limited to 144,000
Lord's evening meal	Annual meeting after sundown to commemorate the death of Jesus
Loving Provision	Rules/doctrine imposed by

	Watchtower corporation

Loyalty	Obedience to Watchtower corporation rules
Loyalty To Jehovah	Obeying Watchtower corporation rules
Marked	When a JW/associate cannot be DF'd or DA'd they are semi shunned
Mature Christian	Obeying Watchtower corporation rules
Meat In Due Season	Dogma from the Watchtower being received
Meek one/s	Those obeying Watchtower corporation rules
Meeting	Gathering for indoctrination
Memorial	Annual meeting after sundown to commemorate the death of Jesus

Mentally diseased apostate	Someone that has left the Watchtower corporation. These 'apostates' must be shunned. 15 July 2011 Watchtower
Ministerial Servants	Watchtower corporation equivalent of a deacon
New light	Changes in Watchtower rules or doctrine
New world	Paradise Earth after god kills all non JWs
New World Translation/NWT	Name of the Watchtower corporation's own version of the Bible
Organisation	Watchtower corporation
Overlapping Generation	Watchtower corporation's own doctrine of what a generation is. It has been invented to justify the end not coming 'soon', especially after the 'generation' they claimed would not die before the end actually DID all die
Paradise (Earth)	Paradise Earth after god kills all non JWs
Pioneer/s	Ones that sign up to do more 'hours' per month in the 'ministry'
Practicing True Religion	Only JWs
Present Truth	Current Watchtower corporation doctrine subject to change
Privately Reproved	Told off for not obeying Watchtower corporation rules
Privilege	A task that furthers Watchtower corporation interests
Public Reproof	Named and shamed for disobeying Watchtower corporation rules
Public Talk	Watchtower corporation doctrinal discourse at the Kingdom Hall

Publisher	One that regularly hands in a 'report slip'
Pure Language	Watchtower corporation speak
Reaching out	Work assignment to a male JW that is doing as much as possible for the interests of Watchtower corporation in order to receive extra 'privileges'

Reinstate/d/ment	Restoration to fellowship after a period of shunning
Remnant	A JW living on Earth, that thinks god has chosen them to go to heaven rather than live on Paradise earth

Report slip	For counting how many 'hours' one spends in the 'ministry'. This is to buy salvation and so the Elders can judge one's 'spirituality'
Revealed Truth	Only Watchtower corporation doctrine
Righteous New Order	Paradise Earth after god kills all non JWs
Righteousness	Obeying Watchtower corporation rules
Satan's System	All of mankind that are not JWs
Serving Jehovah	Obeying Watchtower corporation rules
Sheep	Only JWs or ones aspiring to become JWs
Sheep like ones	JWs obeying Watchtower corporation rules
Shepherding Calls	When Elders visit to 'encourage' underlings
Silver sword	Pet name for the Watchtower corporation Bible. It has a silver/grey cover
Sister/s	Female JW/s (Usually 'baptised')
Slave class	A title (from the JW Bible), that the corporation leaders give to themselves alone
Special assembly Day (SAD)	Large gathering of congregations
Spiritual	Obeying/knowing Watchtower corporation rules, laws and doctrine
Spiritually Unqualified or Not qualified Spiritually	Not obeying Watchtower corporation rules as viewed by the body of Elders
Spiritual paradise	Knowing Watchtower corporation rules, laws and doctrine

Spiritually weak/sick	Not obeying Watchtower corporation rules
Street-Work	'Witnessing' to people in the street
Study	Process of indoctrination using Watchtower corporation publications
Stumble/d	Not obeying Watchtower corporation rules due to being discouraged
Talk(s)	Watchtower based lectures
Teachable	One that obeys Watchtower corporation
Territory	Local area where a JW goes out to do preaching
The Body of Elders	All the Elder in a 'congregation'
The Friends	Only JWs
The Light gets brighter	Justification for flip flops or changes to Watchtower laws, rules or doctrine

The New Order	Paradise Earth after god kills all non JWs
The New System	Paradise Earth after god kills all non JWs
Theocratic	Lit: God ruled. Refers to anything said by Watchtower corporation
The Society	Watchtower corporation and legal entities
Theocratic	Watchtower corporation rules
Theocratic Order/arrangement	Watchtower corporation rules
Theocratic Warfare Strategy	Permission from Watchtower corporation for it's members to lie to non JWs (Watchtower 1 Feb 2007 & Qualified to be Ministers 1967 p197)
Time Of The end	Current period of time. Watchtower corporation say that 'Armageddon' is coming soon
True Christians	Only JWs
Two witness rule	'Wrongdoing' cannot be recognised unless there are 2 or more witnesses or if a confession is made. Sadly, this rule has protected paedophiles and resulted in lawsuits against Watchtower corporation
Undeserved Kindness	Grace, but limited to Watchtower corporation rules
Undeserved/Loving Kindness	Grace, but limited to Watchtower corporation rules
Unity	All obeying Watchtower corporation
Unrepentant	Not obeying Watchtower corporation
Useful Habits	Obeying Watchtower corporation
Waiting On Jehovah	When the Watchtower corporation does not make a law on a subject, a JW must wait. Putting up with injustices in the hope that Jehovah will put it right

Watchtower	A magazine distributed by JWs
Watchtower Study	Indoctrination session
Where the need is great	An where Watchtower doctrine is not widely preached
Wicked System Of Things	All of mankind that are not JWs
World	All non JWs
World Empire Of False Religion	Non Watchtower corporation religions/cults
Worldly	All things Non JW
Worldwide work	Preaching in other countries
Worship Jehovah	Obey Watchtower corporation rules
WTBTS	Watchtower Bible and Tract Society

Zealous	One that obeys Watchtower corporation without question and is proactive in promoting the Watchtower corporation

Ironic Terms used by Ex JWs (mostly)

Most of these terms are self explanatory

A$$emb£y	Assembly
Apathy Trolley/Cart	Watchtower cart/trolley (Where JWs stand next to but do not engage the public)
Arse embly	Assembly
Asleep!	Awake! (Magazine)
Beth-hell	Bethel
Boasting session	Assembly/Convention/Meeting
bOrg	Brooklyn Organisation (Refers to how the Borg take and enslave minds in the Star Trek TV show)
bOrganisation	Organisation (see also bOrg)
Botchtower	Watchtower
Circus Oversneer	Circuit Overseer
Clocktower	Watchtower
CON-vention	Convention

COW	Circuit Overseer's Wife (COW acronym used as a literal word)
Craptised	Baptised
Crooklyn	Brooklyn
Da Troof	the Truth (a term the JWs use for their religion)
Drone/s	JW/s that are totally obedient to the corporation without thinking about any issues.
Dub	Jehovah's witness shortened to JW. From the 'W' = Double u AKA Dub el U
Dublication	Publication (Book, magazine or tract etc)
Dunked	Baptised
Elderette	Elder's wife (Usually attributed to a self important wife)
Eldubs	Elders
Failed Misery	Field Ministry (Door Knocking, proselytising)
Field Serve Us	Field Ministry (Door Knocking, proselytising)
Filthful and Excreting Saliva	Faithful and Discreet Slave (A name the leaders have taken upon themselves to imply Biblical superiority)
Filthful slave	Faithful and Discreet Slave (A name the leaders

	have taken upon themselves to imply Biblical superiority)
Gluttonous Body	Governing Body
Governing Baddies	Governing Body
Happifying	A word Watchtower corporation has used to express happiness. It is an archaic word and thus used ironically, to show how outmoded Watchtower corporation is
Harm N Get 'em	Armageddon
Jah Nuke 'em	Jehovah
Jar Hoover	Jehovah
Jay Man	Jehovah
Jay Dub/J Dub	Jehovah's witness
Je hooba	Jehovah
Je Hoopla	Jehovah
Jehovah's wickedness	JW

Jokehovah	Jehovah
Kingdumb haul	Kingdom Hall
Kingdumb Hell	Kingdon Hall
Kingdumb Maladies	Kingdom Melodies (Cult songs)
Litter-trash	Literature
Mentally Diseased Apostate	Any Ex JW. Taken from a description the Watchtower corporation uses
Ministerial Serpent	Ministerial Servant (Deacon)
New lies	New light
Octopope	When there were 8 members on the Governing Body
Oily Spirit	Holy Spirit
Old lies	Old light
Oversneer	Overseer
Paedophile Protecting Men	Governing body
Piousneer	Pioneer
Popes	Governing body
Prattform	Platform
Rank and file	A name the watchtower corporation gives to their underlings - the average JW
SAD	Special Assembly Day (SAD acronym used as a literal word)
The Lie	the Truth
Theocrapic	Theocratic
TTATT	The Truth about the Truth
Unfaithful and disgusting slave	Governing Body / see filthful slave

Washtowel	Watchtower
Washtowel Babble on Crap society	Watchtower Bible and Tract Society
Watchtarded	Non thinking state of mind of some JWs. Blindly accepting anything the Governing body say, without critical thinking
Watchtower Babylon Crap Society	Watchtower Bible and Tract Society

WBT$	Watchtower Bible and Tract Society ($ used as an ironic way of alluding to the Watchtower being more interested in money than anything else)
Witchtower	Watchtower
Witless/es	Witness/es

The END!

….really!

Printed in Great Britain
by Amazon